STORM OVER THE GILBERTS

EDWIN P. HOYT

STORM OVER THE GILBERTS

WAR IN THE CENTRAL PACIFIC : 1943

 VAN NOSTRAND REINHOLD COMPANY
NEW YORK   CINCINNATI   TORONTO   LONDON   MELBOURNE

Copyright © 1978 by Edwin P. Hoyt

Library of Congress Catalog Card Number 78-7657

ISBN 0-442-80498-9

Printed in the United States of America

Published by Van Nostrand Reinhold Company
A division of Litton Educational Publishing, Inc.
135 West 50th Street, New York, NY 10020, U.S.A.

Van Nostrand Reinhold Limited
1410 Birchmount Road
Scarborough, Ontario M1P 2E7, Canada

Van Nostrand Reinhold Australia Pty. Ltd.
17 Queen Street
Mitcham, Victoria 3132, Australia

Van Nostrand Reinhold Company Limited
Molly Millars Lane
Wokingham, Berkshire, England

16 15 14 13 12 11 10 9 8 7 6 5 4 3 2 1

Library of Congress Cataloging in Publication Data

Hoyt, Edwin Palmer.
  Storm over the Gilberts.

  Bibliography: p.
  Includes index.
  1. World War, 1939-1945—Campaigns—Gilbert Islands.
  2. Gilbert Islands—History. I. Title.
  D767.917.H67   1978b   940.54'26   78-7657
  ISBN 0-442-80498-9

9.00

CONTENTS

MISTAKE AT MAKIN

One sunny July day in 1942, Admiral Chester Nimitz, commander of the U.S. Pacific Fleet, called an obscure marine lieutenant
colonel named Evans Carlson into his office and told him that he
was to make a hit-and-run raid on Makin, an island in the Gilberts
group.

The purpose, said Nimitz, was to secure intelligence about the
Japanese installations, strength, and inclination to fight for the
atolls of the Central Pacific.

The raid, although Nimitz did not say as much to Evans Carlson, was also to be a test of the usefulness of the new marine
raider battalions, which had been developed along the lines of
the British commandos.

Intelligence reports showed that Makin was the Japanese
stronghold in the Gilberts. The islands, however, were supposedly lightly defended. For these reasons Nimitz wanted the
test.

Using old terrain maps and all the available information, Carlson and his men built a model of the atoll. They carefully delin-
eated all the roads, huts, houses, wharves, and tin-roofed stores.
Reconnaissance planes were sent out to make new photos, and
the mockup was changed to accord with them. Nimitz assigned

two submarines, the U.S.S. *Argonaut* and the U.S.S. *Nautilus*, to the raiders, and they boarded and landed from them several times in July. They had already undergone intensive hard training as commando-type fighters. The 220 marines were fit, their morale was high, and they were ready to go by the end of the month.

And so, on August 9, 1942, Carlson and his men embarked from the submarine basin at Pearl Harbor. Carlson's executive officer was Major James Roosevelt, son of the President of the United States.

The submarines were soon at sea, and the men were below, doing more homework for the coming raid. Maps and aerial photographs were distributed, and the men were told for the first time by Carlson that Makin was the target.

There was not much to do aboard the submarines, except eat and sleep, read a bit, study the maps and photographs, and plan their tactics over again. This they did by the hour, peering at the blowups through magnifying glasses, trying to coax from the black-and-white prints every bit of information they could give, trying not to miss a trick.

The voyage took the two submarines a week. They were careful; the object was secrecy, which meant they did not wish to be "spooked" by Japanese aircraft. And so it was Sunday, August 16, when the two submarines lay off the Makin shore.

The plans called for the marines to disembark and get ashore in rubber boats, powered by small outboard engines. They were to be ashore and the boats were to be hauled up on the beaches before dawn (which came at 5:30). They would have the daylight hours to make reconnaissance, attack, destroy the Japanese military installations, and capture prisoners and documents; at nightfall they would return to the submarines.

Carlson himself landed near Butaritari, the major trading community on the island, and headed for Government Wharf on the lagoon side, where the Japanese were supposed to be located.

The landings were rough, but successful. One man accidentally discharged his Browning automatic rifle, and the sputter of its fire alerted the Japanese.

Still, the element of surprise favored the Americans, and they had the assistance of several Gilbert Islanders whom they met quickly after coming ashore. The islanders told them the Japanese were about 200 in number, most of them at On Cheong's wharf and Ukiangong Point.

But it was not as easy as they had hoped. The Japanese were thoroughly alert by 7:00 in the morning and busy at their defenses. The marines were unable to knock out the Makin radio quickly, which meant the atolls of Mili and Jaluit were informed, and news of the raid began moving along the Japanese lines of defense.

By noon, the Japanese were sending over planes to bomb, strafe, and make reconnaissance. When they discovered that the Americans were not there in force, the high command back in the Marshalls relaxed a bit, but the planes kept coming that day, to give as much help as possible to the Japanese garrison.

The fighting was hard going. By 5:00 in the afternoon, Carlson had still not destroyed the enemy forces or most of the enemy installations, he had captured no prisoners, and he had taken no documents. In two hours he was supposed to begin moving out. Next morning he was supposed to make another raid on Little Makin.

But because of the vigorous Japanese defense, Carlson's men were unable to complete their mission that day. They had taken thirty casualties, eleven of them dead.

It was time to withdraw, and so Carlson gave the orders to move to the beach and the boats. He and Major Roosevelt said goodby to the Gilbert Islanders who had helped them. Joe Miller, the chief of police, said he would find the bodies of the dead marines and bury them. The marines gave him guns and ammunition, and by 7:00 they were all down on the beach. Outside the surf lay the two submarines, ready for them to board.

But that night, some of the rubber boats could not get through the surf. The motors broke down, and the boats swamped and washed ashore; the men swam for it.

Carlson and many of his men slept on the beach that night, knowing that morning might bring heavy Japanese reinforcements by air to the island. And then they would face real trouble.

Shortly after daybreak, the Japanese did arrive by air over the island. A flight of Japanese seaplanes came up, hedgehopping from the lagoon to the side of the island where the marines lay.

The delay at least allowed the raiders to move down to On Cheong's wharf and engage in a firefight with a few Japanese. They came back to report that as far as they knew there were no more living Japanese on the island.

They blew up the installations and collected some papers, and to that degree their mission was a success. The body count showed they had killed 200 Japanese defenders, sunk a transport ship, and burned 1,000 barrels of gasoline. But they took no prisoners. There were none to take; the Japanese had not given up.

American casualties were eighteen killed and twelve missing. The latter had disappeared in the difficult attempt to get away on that first night, and were presumed drowned. But they were not —not all of them; they were captured by the Japanese after Carlson left the island, and a short time later were beheaded.

But the rest of the raiders got away in the submarines and soon were back at Pearl Harbor.

There they were treated like conquering heroes. Admiral Nimitz came down to greet them. The press was informed of the "successful mission," and soon headlines were appearing in newspapers all over the world. The war situation was still uncertain that summer of 1942. The Americans had turned back the Japanese tide at Midway, but it was not yet apparent that this was as important a victory as it turned out to be. The fighting for Guadalcanal was furious. The United States needed victories, and these were few and far between.

Thus a minor intelligence raid on a tiny coral atoll in the Central Pacific, in which only a relative handful of men participated, became a "major" victory.

There were medals, including the Congressional Medal of Honor. There was a week at the Royal Hawaiian Hotel, and then the marines were transferred to Espiritu Santu for more training, with the plan to use them in Admiral Richmond Kelly Turner's Amphibious Task Force as shock troops.

They never knew that they had created a storm over the Gilberts that blew all the way back to Tokyo, and that was to have serious repercussions for the Americans.

Two hundred Japanese died in the Makin raid of 1942. But they would be avenged a little more than a year later.

1
THE COMING OF SPRUANCE

When the war was won, the naval historians could all look back owlishly and say that Midway had been the turning point. After Midway the Japanese were on the defensive; after Midway the Japanese expansion drive was stopped.

That turned out to be true, but it might not have been, had affairs gone just a little bit differently at Guadalcanal. There, after the U.S. landings, the Japanese seemed to win all the tactical victories in the beginning, and there were times, such as during the grim struggle for control of airfields and the waterways around the island, when the battle itself seemed lost.

By the early months of 1943, Admiral King and Admiral Nimitz had decided to establish a new striking force in the Central Pacific. The Joint Chiefs of Staff in Washington had created a combined operational command between Admiral Halsey and General MacArthur. The proposed operation down there (New Guinea) did not require the big ships—battleships, carriers, cruisers. They could be freed for other uses.

So Nimitz proposed a new Task Force 50, and the promotion of his chief of staff, Rear Admiral Raymond Spruance, to be its commander.

Spruance was as competent an officer as existed in the navy.

He was Annapolis—Naval Academy—and "regulation" through and through. He was as close to a "fighting machine" as the United States had on its list of senior officers. Unlike Admiral W.F. Halsey, the "Bull of the Pacific," Spruance cared nothing for amenities or publicity. He socialized little and drank less. He was a stickler for detail, but a "big-picture man" as well. His principal claim to fame at this point was his good fortune in being in command of the little American fleet that had defeated the Japanese at Midway on June 4, 1942.

Admiral Spruance was first involved in the planning for the new force simply as chief of staff to Nimitz, but very early in the proceedings it was understood that he would be commander of the operation.

Nimitz needed another fighting admiral. He had Halsey down in the Pacific, and that was all. The others—Ghormley, Pye, Fletcher, Fitch, all names to conjure with from the past—had not proved to have the precise qualities that Nimitz felt were necessary for the job at hand.

Halsey, in fact, did not have them either. In the beginning of the war, he had been christened by the press "Bull of the Pacific," and there was a good deal of truth in the nickname. Halsey fought like a bull, charging forward, and charging again. He also could be a bull in a china shop, with his ready tongue and strong opinions. For the South Pacific, he was just what was needed, a man who could bring out the best in his command, who aroused fierce loyalty in his subordinates, who could charm and encourage the Australians and the New Zealanders, who could arouse Radio Tokyo to spasms of fury with his statements about "Japs," and who could, above all, manage General Douglas MacArthur as well as anyone in the navy.

But Halsey was not a careful man, not a superior planner, not the man to entrust with a delicate mission in which knowing when to stop was as important as knowing when to fight.

Spruance had already shown this knowledge at Midway, when he had turned back from the night chase that would have led him into the jaws of the Japanese fleet. Spruance, then—the man who

eschewed publicity and hated quarrels, the quiet professional—
seemed just the right man to Nimitz to handle the new command.

The task, of course, was to convince Admiral King, a man of
strong mind. But King had one great quality: if he trusted a
commander (and he trusted Nimitz) and had nothing personal
against the man (as he definitely did against some senior officers),
he would generally accede in such matters.

And so, in May, while all these plans about the Central Pacific
were in embryo, Spruance had been promoted to be vice admiral, which put him right up with Halsey and John Towers, the
air commander, and on top of almost all the other officers of the
fleet.

Morning routine for Nimitz and Spruance would begin with
breakfast at the Nimitz house on Makalapa Drive, and then a
walk down to the headquarters building adjoining the Makalapa
compound. Each would go to his office to read the messages that
had come in overnight, and then at 9:00 Nimitz would assemble
the staff in his office for a morning meeting, to review the war
and intelligence reports.

At 11:00, Nimitz received commanding officers. It was his
habit to see every commanding officer of every ship that arrived
in Pearl Harbor. And sometimes there were other callers. Nimitz always tried to have as much contact with the men of the fleet
as he could manage.

Spruance had distinguished himself with Nimitz by his superb
efficiency as chief of staff. Rear Admiral Milo F. Draemel had
been Nimitz' principal aide; he had come to the post from the
job as commander of cruisers in the fleet at the time of the Pearl
Harbor attack. Nimitz had needed an "old fleet man" for the
transition period, as he reshaped the Pacific Fleet from top to
bottom, and Draemal had done his best. He was the battleship
type, tall, even gangling, slow-speaking, deliberate, accustomed
to the old perquisites of rank and privilege, sure in his knowledge of "the navy way." He was a "sundowner" by nature, a
tough disciplinarian during duty hours, a genial companion after.

Then suddenly one day the chief of staff's office was occupied by the short, slender Spruance, whose distinguishing characteristics were a square jaw, clear, unsmiling eyes, and no-nonsense expression. With Spruance one never knew if it was sunup or sundown. It made no difference to him.

As a young man, Spruance took the Naval Academy examinations in Indiana, where his family lived, in the spring of 1903. Just to be sure he took them again that summer while at his grandmother's house in New Jersey. "Sprew" won both appointments. As far as the books were concerned, he was brilliant. After classes and drill he was so shy that his classmates never really knew him, and when it came time to characterize him for his graduation profile in *The Lucky Bag,* the Academy yearbook, all his peers, the editors, could find to say about him was that he was devoted to duty.

When he took over the office next to Nimitz' in the big building at Makalapa, there was a good deal of pushing and shoving, and strange orders to the carpenter's shop.

And then, a few days later, Lieutenant James Bassett, one of the Cincpac public-relations officers, came in on business, and stopped short.

Draemel's office had been undistinguished, but normal enough, with an ordinary desk and swivel chair, and a couple of hard-backed chairs for visitors.

All were gone, Bassett noted with dismay. He could not help but note it, for he looked to see where he would sit down if the admiral invited him to, and there was no place. Worse than that, Spruance was standing at his desk. All that sweating in the carpentry shop had produced a sort of elongated podium, behind which the chief of staff stood, fixing his visitor with a clear blue eye.

Bassett did not stay long. He blurted out his business and fled.

After him for the next six months, hundreds of others did the same. The standards of "business" at Cincpac rose about three notches.

And noting this, when the time came to choose the officer who would lead the new Task Force 50, Nimitz selected Spruance, all without fanfare.

In that beginning of the planning, in February 1943, Nimitz had been most reluctant to think in terms of the seizure of territory. The American comeback was proceeding very well. The production of ships, and particularly carriers, was moving apace. The new *Essex*-class carriers were on the way—a dozen of them. The submarine war was becoming effective, hitting the Japanese in the belly, and decimating their supplies of precious oil. The Americans could afford to wait.

But late one February day Nimitz had the word—action.

He had flown to San Francisco and was driven to the office of the commander of the 12th Naval District. There was Admiral King, the commander-in-chief, with some unsettling news.

The politicians (that meant FDR) were calling for action, King said. If they of the navy did not choose the form and place, the political leaders would choose for them—and that might be disastrous.

And so the wheels were put into motion to bring about the campaign in the Central Pacific.

During the spring, Spruance continued to serve as Admiral Nimitz' chief of staff. There was no point in his being detached too early, during the supply phase. They had to get the material together in Oahu to begin the work.

The project Admiral Nimitz wanted to work on was an invasion of the Marshall Islands. The Joint Chiefs of Staff wanted him to follow this program, and that was understood.

One might say that the Central Pacific campaign began with Admiral King's restlessness. Since the summer of 1942 King had been pressing the Pacific command; he was, in Washington, the most aggressive admiral of the lot. And he was constantly asking for more than the Pacific Fleet could possibly deliver. But through these demands, King got more than the fleet ever thought it could give.

During the Casablanca conference the Americans had insisted

that the Allies pursue the war against Japan, even while making Germany the first objective. Coming home from that meeting, Admiral King wirelessed Nimitz, asking about the possibility of an assault on some islands in the near future.

Nimitz replied that he had not enough ships or enough troops for an assault on anything.

But there were many pressures at work. Not least of them was the ambition of General Douglas MacArthur, who wanted to pursue the war from the bottom up—move from the South Pacific toward Japan. He had no interest in a Central Pacific push, and felt it was a waste of time.

General MacArthur was persuasive, and one of King's major worries was that the navy would be pushed into the background, which it most certainly would have been had MacArthur had his way.

In the jockeying that went on, MacArthur did not have his way, nor did the navy. The Joint Chiefs could only agree to let MacArthur proceed with his campaign in the South Pacific, and let the navy work out its campaign in the Central Pacific.

But the JCS meetings in the winter of 1942–43 made it quite clear to King and to Nimitz that if they wanted to retain any initiative, they had to move, rather than let control of naval operations go by default into MacArthur's hands.

Thus, although Nimitz had said in February that he was not in any way ready for an invasion, by April, when Admiral Spruance returned from Washington with reports of the JCS meetings, Nimitz realized that something had to be done, and done that year.

By June all this was decided. It was also decided that the first strike in the Central Pacific would be at the Marshalls on November 15, 1943.

So Nimitz and his staff began thinking about the coming invasion of the Marshalls. One thing they knew: it would involve an amphibious operation more extensive than anything they had yet tried.

Eighteen months after the beginning of the Pacific war, American shipbuilding and attrition had roughly equalized the sizes of the American and Japanese fleets. However, the Japanese had certain advantages. Their loss of Guadalcanal had relieved them of the need to support the South Pacific operation. That meant their fleet was free to move. Furthermore, the Japanese fleet was moving within an internal zone of communications throughout the Central Pacific and its bases, some of which they had held since the end of World War I. Rabaul in the Bismarck Archipelago, Truk in the Carolines—these were fearsome names, and well might they be. Among other things, they represented Japanese air power. Through the system of island hopping, the Japanese could move aircraft from the homeland manufacturing plants to the Central Pacific islands, entirely by air. The Americans required carriers, but the islands and atolls within the Japanese network of bases served for the Japanese.

The Japanese thus enjoyed a natural air superiority. There was only one way to eliminate that, and it was to seal off any atoll under attack, and keep up constant air and submarine pressure to see that the area remained sealed off.

The Japanese also had certain other advantages. Their fighter planes, the Zeros in particular, were certainly among the best in the world. Their bombers, the famous twin-engined Bettys, were the most utilitarian in the Pacific and were also available in large numbers. The Japanese had maintained control of the sea and the air for most of the Guadalcanal campaign, and they would have all the same advantages anywhere in the Central Pacific. Supply lines were a vital factor, and here all was on the side of the Japanese.

The only answer was to overwhelm the enemy by the creation of a force so powerful that the characteristics of ships and planes and weapons, and even the fighting spirit of the men, would be a secondary factor.

So if the Central Pacific was to be taken on, it must be in a big way, using major forces and establishing immediate air and sea control, and then putting the men ashore with enough equipment and support to knock out the entrenched enemy.

One of the most serious problems was the lack of American intelligence about the intentions and fortifications of the enemy. Only little by little was such intelligence becoming available, in captured documents found here and there that referred either directly or obliquely to events of the past.

For example, the battle of Midway was fought early in June 1942, and Admiral Spruance had turned away at the end of the battle, instead of following the Japanese, whose carriers had been knocked out, and trying to destroy the battleships and cruisers. In analyses prepared for the Naval War College, Admiral Pye, the president, had taken Spruance to task for this, and Admiral King had agreed that Spruance had acted without proper aggressive intent.

It was four months later before Spruance was able, through intelligence officers at Pearl Harbor, to come up with the rebuttal argument: the Japanese had retreated to within the shelter of their main fleet, and had the Americans continued on a westward course (chasing the enemy) on the night of June 4, they would have collided with an overpowering Japanese fleet that included more carriers.

At the outbreak of the war, this sort of American intelligence had been almost nonexistent. The American navy knew virtually nothing about the Japanese strength in the Marshalls, or the Gilberts, or any of the other islands.

Some help had been given when Commander Edwin T. Layton, the fleet intelligence officer, was heard in his pleas in behalf of intelligence. Before Layton's time—indeed, well into the war —fleet intelligence consisted of four officers and one enlisted man to collect, evaluate, and disseminate all that was known about the Japanese. Perhaps it was a proper work force for the load, since U.S. naval intelligence about the enemy was so scanty as to be almost useless.

Now Nimitz had established the Joint Intelligence Center, Pacific Ocean Areas, which set about collecting and evaluating everything possible about the Japanese. Some Japanese language experts were coming out of school—they had to be; the navy had started the war with fewer than half a dozen Japanese experts.

None of this encouraged a feeling of security at Pearl Harbor when the Joint Chiefs spoke about an invasion of the Marshalls, one of Japan's most heavily fortified bases. And when the fleet's war-plans experts came up with a plan to invade Kwajalein, Maloelap, Wotje, Mili, and Jaluit almost simultaneously, Admiral Spruance, among others, said it was suicidal. The Americans simply did not have enough experienced combat troops or adequate means of delivering them to undertake such a scheme. No one could even tell whether these islands were stoutly defended or not, so poor was American intelligence.

Furthermore, said Spruance, the American invasion force would be split into five parts, and as such would be extremely vulnerable to Japanese attack under sea, on the sea, and in the air.

Captain Forrest P. Sherman, who was then chief of staff to Admiral Towers, suggested that the Americans first seize Wake Island. This would have several advantages. The capture of Wake by the Japanese had been a part of the national disgrace of Pearl Harbor, proof of the unpreparedness of the U.S. military establishment for war. Capture would wipe out some of the bitterness of that defeat.

Further, Wake was invaluable as a base. From there planes could fly over the Central Pacific bastions of the Japanese for reconnaissance purposes, and they could most certainly reach the Marshalls, which was the point in question.

But Spruance did not like this idea. He wanted the first attack to be made against a Japanese point that could be used as an air base and as a fleet anchorage. Somehow that argument carried, although it was forgotten in the future planning, because no one ever claimed that either Tarawa or Makin atolls in the Gilberts were ideal fleet-anchorage locations.

But that was the way of the war—ideal arguments were presented, and built up and accepted, and then found to have very little to do with reality. The reality was that the navy had to get on the move or lose its credibility with the Joint Chiefs of Staff

—and thus probably be forced into a back seat in the Pacific war.

The problem was that there was no easy target. Assuming that Spruance was right about the need for an anchorage as well as an airfield, the Marshalls were the obvious choice. But no one knew how well the Marshalls were defended, and no one wanted to find out by attacking blindly.

There were other islands. The only one Americans knew very much about was Makin in the Gilberts, and that was because Lieutenant Colonel Evans Carlson and his raider battalion had made that strange mission to the Gilberts in the summer of 1942 to check out the islands, and also to check out the ability of the marines to carry on the commando-type operations that were so popular in Europe at that moment.

One thing was true: the navy knew something about the beach conditions, water depths, reef locations, and defensive installations of Makin as of a year before. Not all those things would have changed, and the aerial and submarine photographs of earlier times could help in planning. As for the rest, new aerial and submarine findings could be put together this time.

There really was little choice once the admirals and the staffs got down to it. If not the Marshalls, then it had to be the Gilberts. And it had to be something, for Washington was pressing.

Once the decision was made, it had to be justified and amplified.

The Ellice Islands are about 1,000 miles east of the Gilberts. It was barely possible to use them as a base for monitoring the Gilberts by aerial reconnaissance. And land-based aircraft from the islands could provide air support for the amphibious assault troops.

Since the Gilberts invasion was going to be an "easy" operation, it would provide cheap training for the American assault troops and the amphibious commanders, which they would need on later and harder missions in the Pacific.

Nimitz did not like the idea very much, but he had no particular alternative, and he knew better than any of the others that Admiral King would not sit by idly and watch General MacArthur steal the navy show. So Nimitz reluctantly agreed to the Gilberts idea, and in July the proposal was sent to the Joint Chiefs of Staff for approval with all the enthusiasm the navy could commit. It was, perhaps, lucky that military language is so unrevealing.

The Joint Chiefs had what they wanted—action that would preserve them from criticism—and so they approved and directed Nimitz to take Tarawa atoll in the Gilberts on November 15. They would call it Operation Galvanic.

The plan was to be worked out between Spruance and Nimitz, and when the commander of the Pacific Fleet approved it, he would propose it to King.

As usual, King had some ideas of his own. He could see the good sense of trying the easier invasion first, but he wanted more. Nimitz could do it his way, but he should also take Nauru, King said.

Nauru? It was 380 miles from Tarawa, which meant the deployment for a long period of a major part of the naval force and possibly of the air power too. And what was to be gained? Nauru, a phosphate island, was worth little. The Japanese used it as an air base for the observation of the Gilberts and the Marshalls, which was, of course, why King wanted to take it. But it was also very close to Truk, and Truk was the particular problem that vexed Nimitz in his wakeful hours of the night. Truk was the big Japanese naval base, too far from any Allied position for aerial observation. Nimitz' intelligence about Truk was gained through the periscopes of submarines, and the fish-eye view was not an accurate way to measure the enemy's strength.

That strength was considerable, Nimitz knew. He called Truk "the *cojones*" of the Japanese, the source of their power in the South and Central Pacific. He was not eager to stir up the aerial hornets there while carrying out the first of a new kind of amphibious operation on the road back through the Central Pacific.

Back at Pearl Harbor, Admiral Spruance was put to work selecting the men who would serve under him.

First he chose a chief of staff, Captain Carl Moore, whom he had known since early days in destroyers. He trusted Moore—and he showed how much: he left the choice of the rest of the staff up to his new aide.

Then he began choosing the commanders.

First came Rear Admiral Richmond Kelly Turner, the most experienced officer in handling amphibious operations of the modern variety. Turner had put the troops ashore for Halsey at Guadalcanal, and he had met the problem of supplying them under constant fire and aerial bombardment. And so "Terrible Turner" became the amphibious commander.

He was known as "terrible" because of his temper. Vice Admiral Ghormley had called him "somewhat intolerant in dealing with others." It was, if anything, understatement.

He certainly was a Tartar when aroused, but hardly anyone who did not know him could believe that. He was a slender, mild-looking man, neither very tall nor very imposing. But as he had already shown in a number of chores in this war, he was one of the "comers" who could get things done when they had to be done. His assignment for Halsey had involved breaking new ground, finding new ways to deliver men and supplies to islands in the South Pacific, and then planning an ever-growing series of operations against the enemy.

In the middle of July, Rear Admiral Turner was relieved of the South Pacific command and headed for Pearl Harbor. He stopped off for talks with Nimitz and Spruance, and then headed east for California, on three weeks of leave. Then, on August 25, he was back in Pearl Harbor, reporting to Spruance.

At Pearl Harbor, they asked Kelly Turner whom he wanted to command the ground troops in the operation. He thought a time and then recommended Major General Holland M. Smith, of the Marine Corps.

When Nimitz got the recommendation, he might have winced a bit, for he could foresee difficulties. Both Turner and Smith were men of strong opinions, and neither was willing to give in without a last-ditch fight. So there would most certainly be fireworks.

But on the other hand, Kelly Turner must know his man, too, and it was Nimitz' firm belief that a commander should choose his own people. So although the relationship between the amphibious commander and the shore commander was nebulous, Nimitz was willing, and so was Spruance, to let the two officers work it out together. Spruance had wanted Turner because he had high respect for him, going back to the days of the Naval War College in 1935 and 1936 when they had both served there. Turner wanted Holland Smith because he said he was the best man in the country for the job.

So Spruance now had Major General Holland M. Smith of the Marine Corps. He did not "officially" choose Smith—Admiral Nimitz did that job. He called "Howling Mad" Smith out to the Pacific to put him in charge of all the marines in the Central Pacific area. For it had been decided that the marines would be shock troops of the amphibious landings all through the Central Pacific campaign.

Smith was sixty-one years old, and a fine, tough physical specimen of a marine. The year before some of his many enemies had tried to get him retired, but his friends were stronger and managed a transfer to the West Coast, where he trained troops for combat in the Pacific. He first saw the war in the Aleutians, where there was little to see. But he did remember one event: a banzai attack by the Japanese on Attu, where the enemy raged through U.S. hospital tents, killing many of the sick before they were in turn killed. Smith would not forget that banzai attack— it struck him like cold steel—and when he returned to Camp Elliott, California, he made sure his marines destined for the Pacific had extra training to combat just such tactics.

Soon he was in Pearl Harbor, and on a trip with Nimitz to visit the South Pacific, where the men he trained were fighting. Then he went back to his training command, with the understanding that soon he would be brought to the Pacific.

Smith spent more time in the north that year. He went to Adak, to train American and Canadian troops under arctic conditions for the assault on Kiska. There he spent the rest of that summer of 1943, while at Pearl Harbor Nimitz and Spruance planned: it would be the Gilberts—and then the Marshalls.

The Gilberts were vital to control of the Central Pacific, lying north and west of islands held by the Americans, and south and east of the major Japanese bases in the Carolines and the Marshalls. They had been held by the British until 1941. Carlson's raiders landed on Makin and found it little changed. But the Marshalls—there was a different story. The Japanese had taken over the Marshalls at the end of the First World War, and their control was legalized by a mandate from the League of Nations, which formally took the islands away from Germany.

What the Japanese had been doing there was very much a mystery. They had also had more than twenty years to fortify, and it had to be assumed they had done so. Also, the Marshalls were so far from American bases that the observations for intelligence would have to be made by reconnaissance planes from carriers. The Gilberts could be reached by land- or shore-based aircraft from Funafuti in the Ellice Islands, where the navy already had a base.

So the timetable was worked out: the Gilberts to be invaded in the fall of 1943, the Marshalls to be taken in the spring of 1944.

As the reconnaissance began, the Japanese were aware of what was happening. They, too, were making plans.

In the spring of 1943, Vice Admiral Kusaka, the commander-in-chief of the southeastern area for the Japanese fleet, called a meeting at Truk to decide on general strategy of defense. Vice Admiral Kondo of the Second Fleet was the other major party to the meeting.

The Japanese knew they had to expect major Allied assaults on their outer empire. They would reinforce the southern area, in the Solomons, Dampier Strait, and the Bismarcks with as many aircraft as possible. To the Gilberts and the Marshalls they would bring troops from Japan. Thus, with the concentration of the Second Fleet's naval forces at Truk, they would be able to fight any offensive from the Allies in the Solomons, in the Marshalls-Gilberts (as they were termed by the Japanese), and in eastern New Guinea.

As for the Gilberts, if the Americans struck there, as the admirals were inclined to believe they would (for they could think as precisely as Nimitz and Spruance), long-range aircraft would fly from the Bismarcks and land at fields in the Marshalls for gas. They could then operate from the islands.

Short-range aircraft would be brought in stages from Truk and other islands, and would move up to attack. It was expected it would take them four days to reach the fighting area.

As for the surface fleet, Admiral Kondo's ships would move out of Truk and up to attack the Americans as soon as they were notified of the impending invasion. They would strike the invasion forces and knock them off the beaches. Meanwhile, half a dozen submarines assigned to the command would come in to attack the surface fleet and repel the invasion.

On paper, it all looked good.

But the trouble began in April, when Japanese air losses were so severe in the Southwest Pacific that the whole plan was subjected to revision. The planners of the Second Fleet began to talk about moving back to a defensive line at the tip of northern New Guinea, holding Truk and the Marianas, and letting the Gilberts and the Marshalls go. The garrisons would fight, of course, but the fleet would not be risked, nor would any whole effort be made to send large numbers of planes to the islands to fight for them. The plans began to change.

The Japanese had been building defenses in the Gilberts for many months; the real effect of the Makin raid by Carlson's raiders was to alert the Japanese defenders. Hardly had the Americans left the islands in the summer of 1942 than the airwaves to Tokyo were humming with messages. The Japanese high command then began to regard the Gilberts as a point of early invasion, and to prepare their defenses accordingly.

During the latter months of 1942, labor battalions were brought to the islands to dig defensive positions. They brought carpenters, pick-and-shovel men, and cement men, and they set to work. These were Japanese civilians for the most part, preparing defenses for the navy.

In the winter of 1942–43, the high command decided something more was needed. Admiral Tomanari Saichiro was assigned to Tarawa as commander. The Seventh Sasebo Special Landing Force was shipped in February from Yokosuka naval base direct to Tarawa, and in March the 1,500 men of the force began to work.

They brought with them heavy naval guns, and many lighter weapons. They began strengthening the defenses, converting them from dirt and palm-tree revetments to concrete pillboxes. Captain Takeo Sugai was an efficient and hard-driving officer, and under him he had dedicated men—Lieutenant Masahi Okada, his adjutant; Lieutenant (J.G.) Naosuki Tai, the junior adjutant; Dr. Sadao Hagakawa, the medico; Ensign Shinichi Miyamoto; and Ensign Kiyoshi Ota.

For a time the high command sent senior officers to observe and direct, and once even an admiral from Tokyo came to observe their operations.

Ensign Ota's unit consisted of thirty-six men and six boats of the landing-craft size, with bow ramps. They could carry eighty armed men into landing, but now they were used to move about among the islands and bring coconut logs to Tarawa for the defenses. Some 2,000 men were on the island in the springtime, working at good speed to prepare for the invasion that Tokyo firmly expected after the hit-and-run attack of the raiders. A civilian contractor named Suga supervised the concrete work. They were hampered by shortages, but the ships came occasionally, and the work went on.

The workmen built an airfield and hidden gun emplacements. They were very efficient. The call had come that spring for volunteers to perform "hazardous duty in the south," but those who had answered it found their rewards. Life on Betio was good. The defenders had plenty to eat, much of it brought in from Japan. They had all the cigarettes they wanted to smoke, and a sake ration. When one considered that many of the men neither drank nor smoked, there was plenty to keep all those who did wreathed in gray driftlets and happily befuddled during off-duty hours.

And then there was excellent recreation. They could swim on the beaches, and they could fish in the lagoon. Betio had no malaria, and they avoided dysentery by building their outhouses on pilings out over the waters of the lagoon.

They improved the old pillboxes and log emplacements and built new ones. Most of them became physical-fitness buffs, and spent many extra hours building the bunkers stronger than they seemed to need be, just to lift more logs and push around more sand.

And when they were finished, Admiral Saichiro was a happy man. "A million men could not take this island in a hundred years," he told his men proudly. And they believed it.

It was almost as if they knew there on Tarawa and Makin what Admirals Nimitz and Spruance were talking about that spring in the Pacific Fleet commander's house up on the hill at Makalapa. They worked side by side, even when day was done—they simply moved from the office in the old submarine base up the hill to the house, where Perez, the admiral's steward, brought cold drinks and let them relax awhile before dinner.

They took long walks, and swam together in the sea.

And all the while, as they talked about how the invasion would work, an armada was assembling on the West Coast that was more powerful than the entire Pacific Fleet had been two years before.

2
THE FLEET ASSEMBLES

The Japanese attack on Pearl Harbor had been, in a way, a blessing in disguise, for it helped persuade King and Nimitz that the carrier and not the battleship was the weapon to win the naval war. And so, during that summer of 1943, the armada that was being built at home in the United States was centered about the aircraft carrier.

Spruance's naval attack force was to consist of fleet carriers, light carriers, and escort carriers. The battleships would also be there, new fast ones to keep up with the carriers, and old slow ones that had to be used for softening-up bombardment and other secondary tasks. There were to be heavy cruisers, light cruisers, and a whole swarm of destroyers and all the support ships and cargo vessels that it would take to do the job.

To command this force, Nimitz chose Rear Admiral C.A. Pownall.

"Baldy" Pownall was a naval aviator, but of the earliest school. He had graduated in the class of 1910 at the Naval Academy, and he had come up in the days when carriers were just beginning to be developed. He had been through the Billy Mitchell fight over whether airplanes could sink battleships, and he had absorbed the carrier doctrine of the 1920s and 1930s, which

placed the aircraft carrier rather lower than a cruiser on the list
of capital ships.

Pearl Harbor had set the wheels in motion to change that, but
the navy was not swift to change. Admiral William Yarnell, an
early aviation enthusiast, had come out of retirement and was just
now making a study of naval air-power requirements and pos-
sibilities. Not waiting for that, a group of young Turks in the
navy, led by Rear Admiral John Towers, had taken the bit in
their teeth. Towers and others had gone about the country making speeches about the need for naval air power, and some, like
Captain J. J. Clark, claimed that the United States needed 150
carriers to win the war!

Towers in those days before Midway was chief of the navy's
Bureau of Aeronautics. He had been a brilliant and active aviator
since the days when he had been designated Naval Aviator No.
2. But unlike some of the other naval aviators who were admirals, Towers was an aviator first and an admiral second. His
entire life was naval air.

He considered most of the admirals of the fleet to be fud-
dyduddies, and he was not even convinced that Nimitz himself
had a proper appreciation of the need for naval air power.

Towers chafed for a combat command during the first months,
and at last managed to find his way out to Pearl Harbor to
become commander of the air forces of the Pacific Fleet. It was
not a combat command, but it was as close as he could come to
it.

But now, in the summer of 1943, the admirals of differing
views spent a good deal of time arguing over naval tactics. Towers wanted to show the world (and the Japanese) how to win a
war with carriers. He wanted the fast carriers that would soon
be coming out to be used as attack weapons, to knock out the
Japanese strength in the air and on the ground, and pave the way
for landings.

The more conservative Nimitz, and others, thought the carriers must be used with the remainder of the fleet in a less aggressive posture.

What Towers wanted was to have Nimitz put an aviator in charge of the new task force: himself. He saw in the coming Gilberts operation an opportunity for the naval air forces to make their presence and power felt. He was itching to take them into battle and prove the case.

The new fast carriers were coming to Pearl Harbor that summer. In fact, the whole force began to assemble. It was named the Central Pacific Force (later Fifth Fleet) and it consisted of sixteen rear admirals, three marine generals, and two army generals.

The fortunes of the United States had recovered remarkably by 1943, just as Admiral Yamamoto had feared. Long before Pearl Harbor, Yamamoto had suggested that Japan would be wiser not to quarrel with the United States, because Japan could in no way win a war. Now, Yamamoto was dead, ambushed by an American trick in the South Pacific, but his words were haunting all the Japanese naval staff in Tokyo.

For this new fleet alone showed what was to be expected of America in the war to come. There were to be assigned six new attack carriers, five light carriers, seven escort carriers, a dozen battleships, old and new, fifteen cruisers, sixty-five destroyers, and nearly seventy other ships. There were nearly a hundred army bombers, and nearly 300 marine and navy land-based planes, in addition to all the carrier planes.

And on the way to the Pacific would be more as time went on; Nimitz was to have more than 200 ships, 35,000 troops, and all the supplies and weapons that would be needed to do the job.

This was to happen beginning in the summer of 1943, even though the war was still centered on the European front. In other words, what Yamamoto had feared had already come true, less than two years after the beginning of hostilities.

Nimitz now had what he had wanted from the beginning, and a cautious, able commander to entrust with the responsibility.

There were, of course, any number of views as to how the war ought to be fought in the Pacific. But the major quarrel was always between the airmen and the traditional naval officers, who were termed "battleship men" by the contemptuous aviators.

The professional distaste was mutual, and by the time Admiral Towers arrived in the Pacific to command the air forces, it had become a real quarrel. The naval officers, before the war, wore black shoes in winter with their uniforms, and white shoes in summer. But the aviators, with green-and-brown uniforms as well as navy blues and whites, were also authorized to wear brown shoes with the flying-duty uniforms. Thus came into being the terms "brown shoe" and "black shoe" to characterize a whole philosophy of warfare.

The black shoes believed in the essential power of the fleet, built around traditional naval units using traditional naval gunfire as a prime weapon. The brown shoes were the advocates of air power. To them a carrier was not a fleet unit, but a launching pad for air power. For a long time it had been a source of annoyance to the brown shoes that so few of their numbers rose high in naval rank, and that they seldom even had command of the carriers from which they flew.

To be sure, Admiral King, Admiral Halsey, and a number of other commanders of the time were qualified as aviators. But Halsey was probably the worst pilot that ever lived, even though he managed to get his wings (which he did at the advanced age of fifty). And King was even less aviation-minded than Halsey.

So it was, too, with almost all the naval aviator commanders who went into the war. Aubrey Fitch was one of the exceptions; at this time he was commanding land-based naval air for Halsey down in the South Pacific, and he was needed right where he was.

But when the six new attack carriers began to come out to the Pacific during the summer and fall of 1943, they brought with them a group of aviators who were on the verge of promotions to command and flag rank. Under peacetime conditions many of these men would have had to wait another ten years or so to get such commands, but the number of carriers, fleet, light, and escort, meant that men had to be "fleeted up" to high rank for the duration of the war.

Thus, all summer long Spruance planned, and he and his staff argued with various units of the force as to the best use of the whole.

Spruance's chief of staff, Captain Carl Moore, had prospered in the navy until a grim day on the East Coast when he had run his cruiser aground—with Admiral King aboard. He had been a captain then, and as far as King was concerned a captain he would ever be. The grounding of a ship under any but combat conditions was a crime that automatically put a man beyond the pale with King.

And so Carl Moore's career had been ruined. Had there not been a war, he would have retired, and tried to pick up the pieces of his life in civilian surroundings. But it was war, and even though deemed unfit for command, Carl Moore was known as a brilliant organizer and "doer," and besides, Spruance's loyalties went deep, and his relationship to Moore went back to close friendship in Philippines Insurrection days.

Captain Moore's task of selecting all the other members of the Spruance staff shows the sort of commander Spruance was. He was cool and detached, and what he expected from the officers around him was a standard of duty. He had very little interest in them as people; indeed, as a figure, Admiral Spruance was as colorless as a jellyfish. It was unwise, however, for any officer or man to consider colorlessness an indication of weakness. Admiral Spruance was a taskmaster; he did not understand how things could be done the wrong way.

For example, in his choice of aide and flag lieutenant, Spruance went completely out of the pattern of flag officers. It was traditional to choose a "comer," a bright young Annapolis graduate who was, perhaps, the son of an Academy classmate of the flag officer involved. But not Spruance: he chose a former enlisted man, whose main claim to fame was not his dancing, his ability to hold liquor, or his sprightly conversation. Flag Lieutenant E.H. McKissick's main claim to fame was that he had been an absolutely top-grade signalman as an enlisted man. Spruance anticipated that his radio communications might break down in battle, and he wanted a man at his side who could manage the visuals, lamps, flags, and even semaphore, if need be.

In August the carriers were assembling. Two new *Essex*-class carriers were at Pearl Harbor, the *Yorktown* and the *Essex,* and the light carrier *Independence.* They were fast—30 knots and more —27,000-ton ships that carried 360 officers and nearly 3,100 men. They also carried thirty-six fighters, thirty-six dive bombers, and eighteen torpedo bombers. The fighters were the new F6F Grumman Hellcats. The torpedo bombers were the TBF Avengers. The dive bombers were the Curtiss Helldiver SB2cs, and they were the weakest link in the air chain. Soon the commanders of the carriers were replacing them with Douglas SBD Dauntless dive bombers, which were slower, but more dependable.

And the air admirals were also assembling. Rear Admiral Arthur Radford came out to Pearl Harbor this summer, having finished a tour as training officer of the Bureau of Aeronautics. His job was to train the men of the new carriers for battle in the Pacific.

On August 21, Admiral Pownall hoisted his flag aboard the *Yorktown,* and led the new carrier force out for a raid on Marcus Island. This was to be a practice for the coming invasion of the Gilberts.

At dawn on August 23, the ships of the task force made a rendezvous, north of Kauai. The three carriers were there, along with the fast battleship *Indiana,* and the light cruisers *Mobile* and *Nashville.* Ten destroyers and an oiler constituted the rest of the force.

Three carriers! It was the strongest force ever assembled by the Americans in the Pacific. And it was the first time since Midway that the United States had had enough carriers to operate more than one in a task force, a practice the Japanese had carried on since the beginning of the war.

The operation itself, the raid against Marcus, was merely to show what the new force might do. They were heading out 2,700 miles from Hawaii, to a little pinpoint of land only 1,000 miles from Japan. It was an unimportant point, a Japanese weather station more than anything else, but it would do nicely for a test.

The testing went on apace. Captain J. J. Clark handled his 27,000-ton carrier like a destroyer, sliding in and out of formation at flank speed, much to the horror of "Baldy" Pownall, who had been trained in a gentler and more conservative school.

And on the attack, the task force launched its planes in darkness at 4:30 in the morning, again to the worry of Admiral Pownall, who simply did not understand these new tactics and methods of operation.

Because of this, the Americans achieved complete surprise, and strafed seven planes on the airfield at Marcus. They began a shuttling series of raids from the carriers, and before the day was done, they had knocked out an estimated 85 percent of the installations there.

Several American planes were shot down, but as darkness was approaching, Admiral Pownall insisted that the task force move out of the area. He was afraid of submarine attack. His captains were upset because the admiral was steaming off and leaving men in the sea, who might have been saved. They chalked up the incident against him.

When the carriers reached Pearl Harbor again, Captain Clark and several of the others began to complain about Admiral Pownall's leadership. They found ready ears in Admiral Towers, who really would rather have had Pownall's job than his own superior post. But Nimitz was on Pownall's side, for the older man represented "fleet thinking" as opposed to "carrier thinking."

That was to be the point of departure for the aviators, and they were to quarrel along these lines for months to come.

On September 8, Pownall was told by Admiral Spruance that he would be the commander of carriers in the Central Pacific force that Spruance was assembling for the Gilberts attack.

Towers did not like that idea at all. What need was there for a "commander of carriers"? he demanded. The carriers were distributed among the task forces.

So Pownall immediately went to Captain Ralph Oftsie, who

was Nimitz' staff air officer, and opened that battle.

For days the admirals and their lesser officers discussed the employment of carriers. Towers led the airmen.

He told Nimitz that Pownall ought to be commander of one of the task forces, not an air commander or carrier commander for a fleet.

What made Towers and his aviators angriest was the tendency of the nonaviators to think of the carriers as just another kind of ship. For example, one day one of the fleet officers suggested that a carrier be sent to Alaska to ferry some engineers who were needed in the Pacific. One carrier was sent to San Francisco to pick up 5,000 needed personnel. The carrier officers thought this was a base misuse of the finest fighting weapon devised. And they said so.

But Spruance's position was that he was not going to be a guinea pig for the testing of air theories. His job was not to knock out Japanese air power (which the aviators said they could do very soon), or to destroy the Japanese fleet (which the aviators also agitated in favor of), but to take the Gilbert Islands as quickly as possible and with as little loss of life as he could manage.

Nimitz agreed. Towers wanted to use at least one heavy carrier (fleet) and one light carrier in every task force. Only when there were more task forces, said Nimitz.

But in the training of the carriers for the coming operation, Nimitz more or less let Towers have his way.

By midsummer, the Japanese knew that the Central Pacific Force existed, and that it would soon be moving against some point. They were not quite sure whether the target would be the Marshalls or the Gilberts.

The defense plan called for the air forces in Truk to put up an air umbrella over the islands when the time came, and to cover for an area of 50 miles around them.

What was wanted, of course, was troop reinforcements of the area, but the Japanese high command had troops spread so far and wide that it had none to spare. One division of 15,000 men was brought into the inner South Seas area, but that meant it was spread over many islands. So were the handful of planes brought to reinforce the Japanese air forces. No naval units or navy men were sent in at all.

The defense of the area, generally speaking, was the responsibility of the Fourth Fleet, which by this time was basically an administrative unit with two cruisers, three or four destroyers, half a dozen submarines, and a small number of planes.

In July, the Japanese were very much occupied in the Solomons, where the level of activity was increasing constantly. Naval reinforcements arrived in the middle of July, and so did elements of the Combined Fleet, the major striking force of the Japanese navy. They came to Truk.

The Japanese were definitely on the defensive. That month, the cruiser *Jintsu* was sunk off the Solomons, and the cruiser *Nagara* was damaged by a mine at Kavieng. The destroyer *Kawakaze* was damaged by a torpedo from an American submarine. And the destroyers *Mikazuki* and *Ariake* went aground during operations out of Rabaul, and were both sunk by B-25 bombers. The destroyer *Yugure* was sunk off Kolombangara by a combined attack of bombers and surface ships. The destroyer *Kiyonami* was sunk off Choiseul Island.

Obviously things were not going well for the Japanese.

In August the pressure seemed to ease a bit. The Japanese had moved the naval striking force down to Truk, and the major units of the Combined Fleet came from Japan early in August. Some ships put in at the Truk repair base for work, but most of them engaged in training activity, waiting for some U.S. move.

The destroyers were busy carrying supplies and troops to various islands in the South Pacific, to Rabaul and Kolombangara.

In September, when the American carriers attacked Marcus, the Japanese responded by sending the striking force and the diversion attack force out to sea, to look for the enemy. But they found nothing. Several ships were sent with antiaircraft batteries to reinforce Rabaul. The Marianas were strengthened. The Marshalls were strengthened. Only the Gilberts were not reinforced.

Then came raids on Wake, at a time when most of the Combined Fleet was at Truk. The Wake raids brought an alert throughout the area and some changes in the command structure. The main striking force moved to Eniwetok, and then searched for the enemy task force in the vicinity of Wake, by which time the Americans were long gone, had even made their critique at Pearl Harbor, and were looking forward to more operations.

The Japanese were simply waiting for American attack, but they were not sure when or where it would come, and there was little they could do to protect themselves.

In the Gilberts, Captain Sugai speeded up the building of the concrete blockhouses. Ensign Ota's landing craft kept ferrying coconut logs from the outer islands to the Tarawa atoll, which was regarded as a focal point of attack, although it had been Makin where the raiders had landed the year before.

Nimitz and Spruance did not know it, but the aviators had some strong arguments on their side. It was almost as if they could see into the network of Japanese defenses. For at this time, the Japanese were very vulnerable. Had the carriers been thrown against Truk and Rabaul in great strength, they probably could have wiped out the Japanese air power. For this summer, the Japanese high command were prepared to write off Truk, and the movement of the antiaircraft defenses to Rabaul was the proof of it. Nimitz did not know that not only were the AA guns going out, but the big naval guns that protected the harbors were also being transferred to Rabaul. And as for Rabaul itself, at this period it too was "soft," and would have been easy to hurt sorely.

But the Japanese still did not know for sure what was going to happen. The strengthening of the Gilberts in the early part of 1943 had been a precaution; were the Americans going to head for Palau or Saipan?

The guessing was all-important. For here, in the autumn of 1943, a black specter was closing in on the Japanese war effort.

The Combined Fleet, operating out of Truk, was under severe restrictions. Diesel oil was in so short supply that there was none available for maneuvering about the area in which the attacks might come. There could be no brave gestures. The Japanese navy's shortage of fuel had already begun to impair the fighting ability of the fleet units.

3
ENGAGEMENT

In September, the U.S. carriers were on hand, at least enough of them, to try another raid that would be more than an exercise. The carrier men were to get as much information in various ways as they could about the defenses of the Gilberts. They were also to test them and soften them up as much as possible.

In September, the carriers *Lexington, Belleau Wood,* and *Princeton* headed out to make this attack. They would strike Butaritari, the southernmost islet of Makin atoll, and Betio islet of the Tarawa atoll.

The *Princeton*'s story is more or less typical of the attack.

By the night of September 17, the *Princeton* was in position to make her strike. Her skipper, Captain G. R. Henderson, began launching planes at 3:30 in the morning, well before dawn, for the strike on Makin. (The Tarawa strike was launched at 4:45.)

On the Makin strike, two fighters and two bombers set out from the carrier. The bombers were to bomb any ships present, and ground installations if they found no ships. The fighters were to strafe ground installations and aircraft and protect the bombers.

The weather was good. As they came over the target it was still dark, but the visibility was 6 miles, with clouds from 2,000 to 8,000 feet.

The planes flew in over the lagoon, just before 5:00, but it was too dark for perceptive action, so they circled about for a time until the light broke. Then they bored in.

Lieutenant H.W. Crews, in one of the F6F fighters, made four runs over the wharf area, strafing on the fourth run. Then he moved off and let the others work. A little later he came back in and strafed the southeast shore opposite the wharves and circled the center of the lagoon. By this time he saw four flying boats burning in the water.

These had been the target of his more perceptive (or luckier) companion, Ensign L.W. Godson, who was flying the other F6F. Godson had come in and immediately spotted the flying boats bobbing gently in the center of the lagoon at their moorings. He made a pass, firing as he came in low, then zoomed up, came back on the opposite tack, and fired again. The third time he saw the flying boats blazing, and turned away satisfied to return to the carrier—for in the meantime the bombers had done their work. The two bombers were TBFs, flown by Lieutenant Commander M. T. Hatcher and Lieutenant (J.G.) C. C. Dyer. They came in on the same course that Godson had followed, and circled, waiting for the light to come up. When it did, they turned and came back along the south shore, and together turned and made a gliding attack on the installations of the north shore, dropping their four 500-pound general-purpose bombs. Their target was On Cheong's wharf, that point that had been so important for Carlson's raiders to capture a little more than a year earlier.

There were no planes in sight, no ships in the harbor, no sign of life—until the tracers from antiaircraft fire began coming up. But these seemed to do little damage.

When the planes returned to the ship, the pilots of the TBFs learned that they had a few rules to observe: young Lieutenant Dyer had been too close on the tail of Lieutenant Commander Hatcher when they came in, and consequently some of the bomb blast from Hatcher's explosives had come back and damaged Dyer's plane. But it was nothing serious—just something to remember next time.

At 5:00 in the morning another strike was launched from the

Princeton and the *Belleau Wood* against Tarawa. Twenty-two planes set out after takeoff, 92 miles from Tarawa. The formation was ragged because of the darkness and the difficulty the pilots had finding one another. They flew at low altitude and then climbed to 7,000 feet when they were 10 miles off the islands.

Tarawa, the most important island group in the Gilberts, consists of twenty-five small islands. At least they are islands at high tide. At low tide the coral reef between them is uncovered and it is possible to walk from one island to the other. The islands form into an L shape, with a long coral reef underwater that makes a triangle of the L. Inside is the deep lagoon, protected from the sea.

The most important island in the Tarawa atoll is Betio, at the southwest corner of the atoll. The British had built up Betio with housing, warehouses, and a commercial radio station. The Japanese had done much more, as the American reconnaissance flights had observed.

The Americans now moved in, target Betio. Their targets were specified by intelligence and operations: aircraft on the field or in the air, antiaircraft positions for the fighters, and the ammunition dumps and antiaircraft emplacements for the bombers. Maps had pinpointed gasoline and other storage dumps. These were prime targets. They spent about twenty minutes over the targets and did a good deal of damage.

Lieutenant (J.G.) G. W. Spear and Lieutenant (J.G.) F. E. Kroeger went in over buildings near the southeast point of the island, bombed, and set them afire.

Lieutenant John Pincetich took his TBF in at 2,500 feet and dropped four bombs on a heavy antiaircraft gun emplacement. He reported that he had damaged it.

Lieutenant (J.G.) M. Reed bombed a supply area inside the runway perimeter, and it began to blaze.

Lieutenant (J.G.) C. M. Bransfield dropped his bombs on guns and buildings, and then strafed a plane on one runway. The plane burst into flames.

Turret and tunnel gunners of the TBFs also claimed damage

to a PT-type boat north of the long pier, and a Betty bomber on the second runway.

The fighters twisted and turned and zoomed in low to strafe gun positions and barracks and anything that seemed man-made around the airfield.

When they were finished they claimed eight planes destroyed, on the ground. They saw none in the air, except a flight of four Bettys, spotted by Lieutenant (J.G.) H. G. Odenbrett, who saw them just after they had taken off from the runway and moved on a southwest course until they were out of sight. They made no attempt to come back and fight.

The pilots did report that the antiaircraft fire was brisk. But they did not feel that it was intensely strong, nor was a single plane shot down.

The planes flew back to their carriers and gassed up, and several of the pilots went out for another mission just before 9:00 in the morning. Lieutenant Spear's TBF had been hit in the first raid by a shell that entered the nose ring and did some damage. Lieutenant Pincetich's TBF had also been hit by small-caliber rifle and machine-gun fire. These bits of damage did not seem to mean much, and yet on this second mission, the two TBFs found it hard to keep up with the others.

They were back over the target at Betio in an hour, and moved in to bomb. This time they were not so lucky. Lieutenant Bransfield's TBF was hit by AA fire as he pulled out of his bombing dive near the south end of the long pier.

Lieutenant Pincetich, traveling behind, saw black smoke begin trailing from Bransfield's engine. He also saw that the pilot had the plane under control, for Bransfield managed to come down gradually from 1,500 feet until he was about 4 miles off Betio, and then he ditched the plane. Bransfield clambered out, and so did Airmen Second Class J. G. Skinner and J. J. Smith, his crewmen. They got into their rubber boat, pushed away from the sinking plane, and waved at Pincetich and Lieutenant Commander M. T. Hatcher, who zoomed low overhead. They seemed unhurt.

The pilots above reported the position of the boat to the carrier and then headed back to their carriers. Aboard, they found more damage to the planes than on the first mission. This time, as they were debriefed by intelligence, they told of destroying a section of the long pier and firing more buildings and gasoline-storage areas.

This time, too, they had spotted one Japanese flying boat a few miles off Tarawa, but it had made no attempt to attack.

Early in the afternoon, the combat air patrol claimed its first victim of the mission. Four F6Fs were flying above the *Princeton* when radar picked up a blip about 40 miles away, to the north. The four fighters moved out in a broad line and encountered a Betty at 2,000 feet. Lieutenant (J.G.) J. W. Syme made the first attack, a high sidetail run coming in from 1,500 feet. Lieutenant (J.G.) J. D. Madison followed with a beam run almost immediately. Lieutenant (J.G.) J. P. Altemus came in from the tail. Then they milled outward, Madison coming on the tail this time, and Syme coming from overhead. The Betty's starboard engine began to burn, and flames shot up around the cockpit. The pilot took the plane down in a steep glide, but when he reached 50 feet above the water, the Betty exploded, almost in the face of Lieutenant (J.G.) L. W. Haynes, who had come in on the tail.

In the air, the *Princeton* had lost one TBF that day, its crew down in the water just off the enemy shore, after they had shot down one Japanese bomber.

It had been a tradeoff, speaking in tactical terms. Speaking strategically, the Japanese on Tarawa now had a good indication that they were going to see more of the Americans. They pulled their resources together and waited.

Back at Pearl Harbor, Admiral Towers continued to agitate for more freedom for his carriers to return again and again to the atolls of the Central Pacific, to wipe out all possible Japanese air power as soon as possible.

But the deck-bound admirals did not agree to this plan, and as long as they felt they needed the kind of air support the carriers could give, Nimitz was inclined to let the ship men have their way.

So Towers retired to lick his wounds, and to complain to James Forrestal, his friend and the Undersecretary of the Navy, that the airmen of the Pacific were being badly misused, and that this was lengthening the war measurably.

The meetings in Nimitz' office at Pearl Harbor were beginning to be very testy indeed. Towers wanted the carriers to go out on raids against Japanese targets for training—and to show the fleet admirals just how effective his air power could be by itself. Spruance said these raids would interfere with his fleet training program. He was trying to hone that fleet into a fighting unit that would work smoothly when the landings at the Gilberts began.

Towers argued that they needed more reconnaissance of the Gilberts. But Spruance said he would get along without it.

And then Towers threw caution to the winds and said the Gilberts operation was a waste of time, a case of using a sledge-hammer to drive a carpet tack, and the conference of admirals and staff members broke up into a handful of minor arguments about air power.

Matters were really getting out of hand.

In a way, Towers was securing what he wanted. On October 5, Rear Admiral A. E. Montgomery led a task force of three large and three light carriers against Wake Island, again in what was ostensibly a training operation, but was also for the aviators an opportunity to show how powerful their weapon could be.

Again the carriers launched before dawn. This time the Japanese were alert. Their radar had caught the planes coming in, and they had put up an air screen of some thirty fighters over the island as the carrier planes came to attack.

But the odds, of course, were heavily with the attacking Americans, who had more than a three-to-one margin against the Japanese. So soon the Japanese air power was knocked out of the air, and the Japanese bombers on the ground were strafed and bombed and wrecked, while the Americans lost only a handful of planes.

The carrier force continued its devastating operation. In the afternoon, the Japanese sent help from the Marshalls—two flights of planes, six fighters and six bombers in each flight. They engaged, many of them were shot down, and the rest landed on Wake.

By the end of the day, when the battle ended, the Americans had won a victory, although not a cheap one. The Japanese had shot down eleven carrier planes, but their defenses were hard hit.

Next day, unlike their procedure in any operation of the past, the Americans remained in the Japanese waters and attacked again. At the end of this day there was nothing but light antiaircraft fire left to oppose them. The surviving Japanese planes had fled back to the Marshalls rather than risk destruction at a time when Japanese air power was beginning to wane rapidly.

After the raid on Wake the carrier men were confident that they had proved beyond doubt what they could do.

So it was with hurt surprise that the carrier captains and admirals came into Nimitz' office for a critique of their grand victory —and discovered that the battleship admirals still insisted on relegating the carriers to a secondary role in the Gilberts invasion, as secondary "artillery." The old routine would be followed: the ships would stand offshore, and the battleships and cruisers would strike the beach and the enemy installations with naval gunfire. That was how it had been done since the days of Nelson, and that was the proper way.

The carriers would remain outside, screened by the destroyers and the cruisers, and make air strikes when they were called upon to do so.

This argument was in full swing when Admiral Forrest Sherman brought forth pictures to show what had been accomplished in the air strikes on Marcus and Wake—but he did not win a victory. All he received was some grudging admiration for the carrier effort.

Carrying the argument, Spruance did not want to let the carriers go into the Marshalls to attack before the Gilberts operation —because, he said, it would "tip the mitt" and tell the Japanese that something big was afoot. (The Japanese already knew that much.)

Fired by their own vehemence, the aviators in Nimitz' command pressed their luck. Admiral Aubrey Fitch, who had commanded the *Lexington* task force when she was sunk in the battle of the Coral Sea, suggested that the carriers ought to be used more aggressively than Spruance wanted to use them.

That motion was seconded noisily by Admiral John Hoover, the commander of land-based air forces, and by several of Nimitz' staff members.

Admiral Towers was the one who went too far. He had gone off to the West Coast on navy business, and when he returned, he saw how the wind was blowing. He wrote several letters to Nimitz, the gist of which was that he, Towers, was much better fitted to be task force commander than Spruance.

That move nearly wrecked Towers' career. Nimitz seemed ready to ship Towers out; he even suggested that Towers might choose to go to Espiritu Santo and take command of the air forces in Halsey's area.

For Nimitz knew one thing: the carriers might be ready for all kinds of brave derring-do, but the rest of the ships of this new fleet were not. They were untried, and so was the whole concept of the landing force. And while the Gilberts appeared to be a gnatlike target for the shotgun's aim, such a situation would suit Nimitz.

The naval forces needed some inexpensive experience, and from what Nimitz knew of the Gilberts the cost there would not be too great in men or materiel.

As for the air command, the attitude shown by "Baldy" Pownall—conservative to a fault—was just what was wanted for Spruance's kinds of operations with the carriers.

So the task force was assembled: six heavy or fleet carriers and four light carriers, indeed a heavy weapon to use against gnats.

4

OCTOBER PLANNING

During the daylight hours, Admiral Spruance spent a good deal of time roaming in the hills. He had always been a walker, and now he took hikes for which he became famous at Pearl Harbor, exhausting those of his staff who were unlucky enough to be dragged along. Usually his companion was Captain Moore. His staff labored over the plans for the coming operation in the Gilberts. Spruance would not be pinned down by detail, and Chief of Staff Moore came back from these excursions to join his subordinates and work far into the night. Spruance would have nothing to do with night work.

In the planning stage, everything was considered, from the amount of ammunition to the character of the tides. The tides were an important matter, because Tarawa was surrounded by the coral reef, and that could mean trouble. During the planning stage, a group of Australian and New Zealand officers came to Pearl Harbor to work with the intelligence officers and engineers.

The boats should get in to land at about 11:15 in the morning. The experts predicted that there would be adequate water on the reef for the landing craft. A coxswain could expect to have 18 inches of water under the keel of his LCVP when he came in across the barrier reef; the boat would draw about 3½ feet, loaded, and the estimate was that there would be 5 feet of water over the reef.

Allowances were made. The tides at this time of year might vary, but they certainly should not vary more than a foot. And so, even at worst, the coxswain should have 6 inches of water to float him over the reef from that edge, somewhere between 1,100 and 800 yards out.

Spruance was considering all aspects of the operation. His responsibility was to be sure that all of it went right: the merging of air power, bombardment, troop movement, troop support, and the final part, the assault by the troops themselves. That, in a way, was the icing on the cake—the actual capture of the objectives. Assuming that all went well beforehand, it should be relatively simple.

On August 15, before all the details about the components of the force that would land in the Gilberts had been determined, Admiral Spruance and Captain Moore had flown out from Pearl Harbor on an orientation mission. Spruance wanted to learn everything he could about the war against the Japanese from those who were actually fighting it. He visited Halsey and spoke with several of his subordinate commanders.

Two people he wanted to talk with in particular: Major General Julian C. Smith, commander of the Second Marine Division, which would invade Tarawa atoll; and Rear Admiral Harry W. Hill, who would command the amphibious force that would take the ships to that string of islands.

Spruance had seen them, talked to them, and assured himself that they were the men he wanted. It was not too late yet, if he had some reservations, to make changes. But Julian Smith was an alert and extremely competent marine officer, and Harry Hill was one of the "comers" among the younger men who had recently achieved flag rank. Tall, friendly in manner, he was still a stickler for detail, and a constant searcher for new ideas, new ways to approach the task of landing, defending, and supporting troops ashore.

Spruance's staff realized that the landing craft would probably ground somewhere near the shore. Or, as Vice Admiral George C. Dyer wrote wryly some years later, "It was obvious that it was not anticipated at the command level that the LCVPs would land any marines dry shod."

Before the operation, one of the old Gilbert Islands hands who had come up from Australia had some second thoughts.

It might be worse than they expected, he warned. It might be that there would be no more than 3 feet of water over the reef on November 20 at the hour the landing boats were supposed to come in. Would that make a noticeable difference?

Would it? Indeed it would. The LCVPs then could only shuttle troops in close to shore, and they would have to be taken the rest of the way in by the LVTs, which had a shallower draft.

That was a disturbing thought. It meant all kinds of delays, and difficulties in bringing in supplies and the later waves of men.

One idea was advanced: why not delay the whole operation until November 27 when the tides were bound to be at their highest?

But that idea was rejected. The Joint Chiefs of Staff were already setting up the timetable for the Marshall Islands invasion, which was in the planning stage. They could not delay. There would not be enough time if they did. The invasion must come on November 20.

Then could they not land at dawn?

No, for that would mean there would be no time for the devastating naval gun barrage to be laid down in the morning before the landings. The troops would lose the value of that gunfire, which was expected to knock out the defenses and leave the Japanese reeling, easy prey.

How about the night before, or late in the afternoon when the tides would be higher for certain?

No, said the gunnery experts. Again there would not be enough time then for the men to benefit from the naval gunfire or close air support before dark.

And so, in the interests of the gunnery support, a late-morning assault was chosen.

A great deal was hanging on the performance of those guns.

The first element, Spruance believed, was to achieve surprise. With the photographic operations of American planes in the Pacific atolls, the Japanese must certainly know by this time that something was afoot. And if they had no other sources, it was known that Japanese planes managed flyovers of Pearl Harbor. In addition, it was assumed that Japanese submarines also had made observations, just as the U.S. submarines were doing in Japanese waters.

Yet if the plans were kept secret, then the element of surprise should be achieved. One factor militating in favor of this resulted from the indecision that had been shown earlier: because Nauru, the Marshalls, and even Wake had been considered, their names had been bandied about, and reconnaissance flights had been made. So the Japanese would gain little by watching air activity.

Therefore, since the Gilberts were in no way a major Japanese naval base, Spruance could and did assume that the enemy fleet would not have to be dealt with immediately. There could be no conceivable reason why it should be any closer than the Marshalls.

Once the American force was off the Gilberts, however, the Japanese fleet would doubtless move. It certainly had that capability; it might even attack while the Americans were in the midst of the operation.

This amphibious warfare was all new. Kelly Turner's operations in Guadalcanal had been amateurish next to what was expected here. Turner—and everyone else concerned—had learned a great deal in the failures of the South Pacific campaign, the disastrous battle of Savo Island, the war of attrition in "the slot," that narrow strait where so many American ships now lay on the bottom, and the Japanese control for so very long of the air over Guadalcanal. These tragedies had taught their lesson.

Spruance's major concern was the inexperience of the forces he would lead—including himself—in what was after all a whole new sort of warfare.

He would have surprise. He was sure of that. He would also need speed of operation. That would have to be provided by

Kelly Turner's know-how and good management. The ships had to be on target on time, the bombardment had to be laid down on schedule, the air cover had to be complete and the air raids just right, and then the troops had to be gotten ashore in a hurry and the naval vessels freed for whatever might come.

And the third factor was the protective umbrella to be supplied by the carriers.

That meant, from all the carriers, more than 700 planes of all sorts, plus land-based air, which included patrol bombers, marine planes from the Ellice Islands, air force planes from the VII Air Force—in all, more than 1,100 airplanes.

The fast carrier task force would now consist of eleven carriers, more than any navy had ever put into action at one time in history. Besides that there were the three escort or "jeep" carriers commanded by Admiral Mullinix for direct support of the Makin operation. Spruance would draw this carrier net tight around him and dare the Japanese to penetrate it.

As a naval traditionalist, Admiral Spruance was imbued with that dogma the airmen called "gun-club philosophy." He believed that a fleet, including carriers, was vulnerable to attack by land-based dive bombers and torpedo planes. It was a relatively new concept—the navy had fought the idea that planes were important at all for a long time.

The plans called for the Americans to land at dawn in the Tarawa atoll and at Nauru. That argument was still being carried on in the staff meetings in Nimitz' office, even as the vehicles and guns were assembled and the men were trained for the assault.

There were still many dissenters to the plans. The airmen had been so noisy about so much that their objections were discounted, perhaps unwisely. Holland Smith joined them, for he felt it was most ill-advised to take the Gilberts—and unnecessary. How much better it would be, he said, to move straight in to Kwajalein, the center of the Marshalls. His point, and that of other objectors, was that the Gilberts had virtually no strategic value. If the United States needed an advanced base, it was in the

Marshalls, not in the Gilberts. The Gilberts did not threaten American communications—so why bother with them?

They had no harbor, the Japanese did not even seem to pay much attention to them, they had no fleet value.

But Operation Galvanic had been ordered by the Joint Chiefs of Staff, and it would proceed.

Kelly Turner would command the Northern Attack Force, and Rear Admiral Harry S. Hill would command the Southern Attack force. The northern force would move against Makin. The southern force would take the more difficult terrain of Tarawa—more difficult because Betio, the major base, was small, and the defenders were obviously highly concentrated there.

Holland Smith went to V Amphibious Corps headquarters in the Marine Barracks in the Navy Yard at Pearl Harbor, and began consulting with the staff he had picked for himself. Colonel Graves B. Erskine would be his chief of staff. He learned then definitely that he would have the Second Marine Division, under Major General Julian C. Smith.

For the second assault (which everyone knew would be easier), Nimitz had settled on Major General Ralph Smith's Twenty-seventh Army Division. This division was a New York National Guard unit.

At that moment the Twenty-seventh Division was scheduled to make the Nauru attack. But when Holland Smith studied the intelligence estimates, he was more certain than ever that it was going to be too expensive in time, men, and material to take Nauru.

Holland Smith was not very happy with having to share the operations with the army leaders. In the first place, he had no administrative control over the Twenty-seventh Division. It was trained by the army under Lieutenant General Robert C. Richardson, the commander of army troops in Hawaii. The division and General Smith were responsible to the army. They would be under the command of "Terrible Turner" from the time that they boarded ship until they landed ashore and General Smith could report the beachhead secured. Then the army forces would be under command of Holland Smith as long as they were involved in the operation. The moment it ended, they would revert to the command of the army.

What this meant, in essence, was that Holland Smith had all the responsibility for the division's actions under fire, but none of the authority to supervise its training or to make changes after the operation in case they were needed. It was a most unsatisfactory command arrangment, and was brought to a simmering boil right in the beginning.

Almost immediately matters grew worse. Holland Smith's staff planned both operations and put through the plans for the Nauru landing. They were cleared by Turner and Spruance, and finally they went through General Richardson's office from which they emerged. Richardson then decorated the members of his staff for the "massive planning" of the Nauru operation. When the marines heard about it, their lips curled.

Soon enough, Smith became aware of the army men's deep-seated resentment of the role to be played by the marines in the Central Pacific. Richardson wanted to be in the Central Pacific what MacArthur was in the South Pacific. But Nimitz made very certain that the overall command would be in his hands, and that is obviously one reason why he chose a marine officer to manage the landings. He would be able to maintain this state of affairs throughout the campaign.

For the moment, however, Nimitz felt that he was safe with his marine forces, and he was not at all sure of the fighting abilities of the national guardsmen from New York.

Nor was the quarrel with the army the only one brewing. Kelly Turner was a square-jawed, stubborn man who wanted to do things his own way. He proposed to Admiral Spruance that since he was in charge of the amphibious landing, he should have authority over the marines in training for the Gilberts invasion.

Smith won that battle, by going to Spruance himself. But Turner had managed to persuade the operations officers to leave Smith off the roster. Smith was not going to go along. He was to be left back at Pearl Harbor in technical command, while Turner ran the show.

When Smith learned of this move, he went charging over to Spruance's office. Spruance knew nothing about it. Turner said he had not done it. Nor had he; the culprit was Charles H. McMorris, the chief of staff to Nimitz, who had the old black-shoe battleship man's concept; all naval operations are navy shows.

As Smith put it later, it seemed a wonder sometimes that the Americans were able to fight the Japanese at all in the early stages of the war, because they spent so much time fighting the brass hats of a different era.

Battling continued over details, such as the matter of amphibious tractors to bring the men in from the ships (which was a major issue all the way) and even who was in command of what, and when.

The matter of command was a real problem. Already in the Guadalcanal fighting, the Americans had learned that divided command or uncertain command could be dangerous, even disastrous. Several operations in the South Pacific had floundered because command authority was not properly understood or even stated. Amphibious warfare was a new idea to the Americans; they had to get used to it.

And here, in the Gilberts invasion, Spruance would be working with elements of the army, the army air forces, the marines, the navy, and naval air (carriers); some of the admirals believed the latter sometimes acted as though it were a force all by itself.

All these command problems were worked out not by Spruance, but by his chief of staff with Spruance's authority behind him. Spruance was in charge; under him Kelly Turner was in charge of all operations, which meant those of the force that would invade Tarawa, and that which was originally scheduled for Nauru (later moved to Makin). When everybody got on the ground, Holland Smith would take over the command of the land forces, from Turner. But Turner would still be responsible for the naval forces at sea, and the air forces everywhere. And although he would personally command the amphibious landings in one place, he would also be responsible for Harry Hill's force, which would hit Tarawa.

Hill, in turn, was in command of Julian Smith's Second Marine Division, which would land on Tarawa, except that when Smith landed and took up his command there, he was in charge, and then responsible to Holland Smith.

And at the other island, General Ralph Smith of the army would be responsible to Holland Smith, too.

Just because all these men wore the same U.S. insignia did not mean that they thought alike. Indeed, the differences and jealousies among them were profound, particularly between the army and the marine corps on the one hand and the marine corps and the navy on the other (to say nothing of the airmen and the surface seamen).

To sum up their quarrels:

General Holland Smith resented being placed under command of the navy, even for a moment. It was his idea that marines were taken places to fight. From his point of view, it was nice of the navy to offer the transport, but once the marines had arrived and the barrage had been laid down, they should get off the ferry boats and be left alone, supplied properly, and urged to get on with their job in the best way they knew how.

Major General Ralph Smith, the army commander, was not happy about serving under a marine general, for the army considered the marines to be a Fancy Dan outfit, more fitted for leading dress parades than anything else. In the Pacific, the army had particularly strong feelings about the marines after Guadalcanal, and all the publicity they had received. Further, the army commanders really believed the whole land war ought to be their show. Down south, General MacArthur had made that stick in the South Pacific. Here in the Central Pacific every commander from General Richardson down felt that it ought to be the same.

Admiral Towers, the air commander, was not at all happy that Spruance had the command of the new force. He wanted it desperately for himself, a chance to show Washington just how fast naval air could wrap up this war in the Pacific if given the freedom to do so.

Admiral "Baldy" Pownall, who would be in charge of the

carriers as a force, was not very happy with his own position. He was an airman, but not a modern one. He knew that the young Turks, the carrier captains who had come up through the squadrons, such as Arthur Radford and Jocko Clark, were behind him —indeed they were, and seeking his scalp.

As for the plan, when it was completed, with all its pages and pages of details (dozens of pages, for example, dealing with communications problems alone, because there were so many different units and types of forces involved), General Holland Smith and Admiral Turner saw it for the first time.

Smith studied the section that dealt with the intelligence appraisal of Nauru's strength. The intelligence reports showed that Nauru was a tightly defended place, and that the taking of it would be a tough job. He was committed to the use of the army troops in this second invasion—there were not enough marines to go around, for one thing—and he had no confidence in the army troops at all. It was not that he didn't like army men, he said; it was just that the forces that would serve under Ralph Smith had not been trained yet to do the job.

So Smith complained to Turner, and surprisingly, in such a matter Turner was willing to give way to his judgment. Agreeing that Nauru was too tough a nut to crack, the general and the admiral went to see Spruance.

And Spruance agreed too, although for different reasons. Spruance had never liked the Nauru plan—that was the idea of King and the people in Washington. From King's point of view, Nauru was a worthwhile target because it was so close to Truk, and they might be able to knock off the big naval base of the Japanese by use of land-based air alone after the airmen were established on Nauru. But 380 miles, going in, would be a very tough situation for the attackers, because the Japanese would mount a strong air defense from Truk. Spruance did not relish the idea of swarms of Bettys overhead carrying deadly torpedoes, and protected by busier swarms of Zeros.

Another objection from the strategic or high-command point of view: Nauru and Tarawa were so far apart that if the Japanese committed their main fleet to the operation, and split the attack, Spruance did not feel capable of covering both areas. That would have been argued by the airmen, who held that there was no need for much trouble if they could just be turned loose to crack the Marshalls, Truk, and the rest by themselves. Then moving into the islands would be easy. Spruance had heard these arguments in the meetings of Nimitz' staff, but for a commander who had made his reputation by the daring use of air power at Midway, Spruance had less understanding and appreciation of carriers and their potential than seemed possible. He was still a traditional naval officer, and he thought about fleet units, battleships, cruisers, and naval air as an adjunct of power.

If Tarawa and Makin were the targets, the main American fleet, the carriers, and the fast battleships and new cruisers could be concentrated in one place and then sent out to meet any enemy movement of the fleet.

With those objections plus the objections of Smith and Turner in hand, Spruance went to see Nimitz, and was at first greeted with skepticism.

The fact was that Nimitz knew how King hated to be crossed. The plan for Nauru had come from King and the JCS, and King had had enough trouble getting a Central Pacific drive going in the first place to not want any complications. So Nimitz stalled.

General Holland Smith, on Spruance's request, wrote a letter to Turner complaining that he did not have enough troops to take both these places, and besides that, even if he did get some more troops, the navy did not have the transports to move that many men about.

All this was in the works when Admiral King arrived in Honolulu for one of his infrequent trips away from the U.S. continental limits. Usually the King-Nimitz meetings were in San Francisco, but this time King was persuaded to come out and inspect, to see what was developing in this part of the world.

The meeting began in the Cincpac conference room, and at one point, the lesser admirals and generals of the staff were assembled. Pointedly, in King's presence, Turner passed to Spruance General Smith's letter, with his own approval on it, and Spruance, as if he did not know what it was all about, read it and passed it to King.

King, stone-faced, read it. He turned to Spruance.

"What do you propose to take in place of Nauru?"

"Makin," said Spruance.

So far, so good. The conference went on to other matters, and the Gilberts plan was put aside. In King's mind, the invasion was as good as done. The only trouble was that it was already October, and the plans were not even finished yet.

5
PRELUDE

The aviators at Pearl Harbor were still arguing for strong air strikes against the Japanese air bases in the South and Central Pacific. Towers and his officers told the story of the *Yorktown*'s experience in the Wake raid, hoping it would help make their point.

The *Yorktown* had been steaming in when Lieutenant (J.G.) Charles Ridgway, the fighter director officer, saw two flights of Japanese planes coming in on the radar. They were moving fast down from the Marshalls. The American combat air patrol circling above the carriers was vectored out immediately to intercept, did so, and shot down ten of the twelve planes right there. This was the proof for the unbelievers. Let the carriers out to fight. They knew how to take care of themselves.

Admiral Towers and his assistants tried to argue the case. Admiral Pownall and Admiral Radford went to see Spruance, to present the case for freeing the carriers to hit all the air bases anywhere within striking distance of the Gilberts.

No, said Spruance, he still wanted the carriers to stay in close support of the landings.

The pair went back to Towers, and wanted to go to Nimitz, but Pownall, the more conservative, then said he thought it would not be a good idea to go over Spruance's head that way.

So they continued the struggle in the staff meetings at Pearl Harbor.

Nimitz was sick in the middle of October—otherwise the airmen might have done better. As it was, with the admiral in the hospital, Chief of Staff McMorris held the floor, and he had neither the authority nor the inclination to make a radical decision.

Towers argued the case again in the staff meeting of October 17, to no avail, because although Spruance appeared receptive, "Terrible Turner" said absolutely not: he was entrusted with getting the troops ashore, and he wanted those carrier planes flying that air umbrella above them.

Towers got nowhere with his claim that if the Japanese air power was wiped out beforehand, on the fields and above the islands all around the area, there would be no need for an air umbrella.

The airmen lost the battle. But they gained an important concession. For they would have their own task force, Task Force 50, under Admiral Pownall, and it was to be something new.

The task force consisted of four groups. Three of them each had three carriers; Admiral Sherman's group, called the relief carrier group, had only two carriers. Eleven carriers in all, then, made up a striking force that could really strike—and the men of those carriers wanted to show what they could do.

But Kelly Turner and Holland Smith wanted the planes overhead to support them when the time came. And that was the way it was going to be.

After these arguments with Towers and the other airmen, in which Kelly Turner was the chosen protagonist of the fleet-umbrella theory, Spruance did compromise. He could see Turner's point of view—Turner was the creature of his experience, and at Guadalcanal, Japanese air superiority had cost him dear. He had no wish to repeat the dreadful experience.

But Spruance could see that in spite of their personal differences, and Towers' envy of his new job, the airmen did indeed have a powerful weapon in the fast carrier force. Then let them use it, before the invasion. Let them hit the Marshalls and other Japanese bases, knock out as much of the enemy's air and sea power as they could, and then do what Turner wanted during the actual operations—remain on tap to repel all comers.

Nimitz agreed with this approach, Spruance had his way, and the airmen retired grumbling, furious and certain that they could shorten the war immeasurably if allowed to roam at will, plastering all the Japanese air bases within any sort of range of the Gilberts.

Privately, Admiral Towers was in close touch with Undersecretary of the Navy James V. Forrestal, and Assistant Secretary Artemus Gates, both of them sympathetic to the airman's view.

Forrestal agreed with Towers, and he had little use for the old naval philosophies. But this was not the time to raise the issue. He counseled Towers and the young Turks to go slow. It was hard: the fast carrier force had grown so large that Pearl Harbor could not accommodate them all. They would have to meet at sea.

So the plan was laid down: each carrier task group would be assigned to a particular defensive sector, and they were to intercept flights of Japanese planes, thus supporting the marines.

Task Group 50.1, the *Yorktown,* the *Lexington,* and the *Cowpens,* under Rear Admiral "Baldy" Pownall, would be the interceptor group to stop the Japanese from the Marshalls from attacking the assault forces at Makin and Tarawa.

Task Group 50.2, the *Enterprise,* the *Belleau Wood,* and the *Monterey,* would be under Rear Admiral Arthur Radford, and it would support directly the Makin operation.

Task Group 50.3, the *Essex,* the *Bunker Hill,* and the *Independence,* would be under Rear Admiral A.E. Montgomery, and it would support the Tarawa landings.

Task Group 50.4, the relief task group, the *Saratoga* and the *Princeton,* would be under Rear Admiral Frederick C. Sherman. It was the reserve—if somebody got in trouble, Freddy Sherman would come to the rescue.

The compromise was made, but the aviators bristled, for they claimed that Spruance did not understand air power, and that he did not even have a man on his staff with any influence who understood it either.

It was true. The single aviator on Spruance's staff had no part in the planning, and no one consulted him about much of anything. "Baldy" Pownall, whom Spruance had accepted as his chief air officer in the operation, was the least aggressive of all the air admirals available to him.

But that was the way it was to be, for when Spruance took his completed plans to Nimitz, the commander-in-chief pored over them, asked questions, and approved them. It was settled. There would be no more room for argument about anything.

One of the most serious problems still facing the Americans at Pearl Harbor, in these last days before the Gilberts operation was to kick off, was a paucity of information about what they would face.

No one in the American forces knew much about Tarawa. They had air photographs, but they were remarkably unrevealing. The charts were old, and the Japanese had been in possession of the area for a year and a half.

They did, however, have a good idea of the kind of troops they would face. Captain Sugai's branch of the Japanese naval service —the Special Naval Landing Force—was the equivalent of the marines. These were the Japanese shock troops, and they could be expected to fight for every inch of the ground of little Betio.

As for Makin, it ought to be a soft and easy job of conquest. The main island of Butaritari was held by 290 combat men and 271 laborers. All Holland Smith believed he would need to take Makin was a single regiment of army soldiers, the 165th Regiment.

Holland Smith was still uneasy about the army, but knew that at least this regiment was the best in the division.

One tends to think of an amphibious operation as starting from Point A and going directly to Point B, but the Gilberts operation did not work that way at all. The Second Marine Division embarked direct for Tarawa from New Zealand, while the Makin forces sailed from Pearl Harbor, along with Task Force 50.

Before the operation, there were still many disagreements about procedures and equipment—Holland Smith's demand, for example, for amphibious tracked vehicles to take his marines ashore. The navy wanted nothing of the kind. The LCVPs (landing craft, vehicle, personnel) and the LCMs (landing craft medium) should be adequate for the job, said Turner. But Smith worried about underwater obstacles and barbed wire that might hold up the ramp-equipped landing craft, and he knew that the amphibious tractors could make their way through and over these. He wanted to land his men in amtracs for the first three waves, and then bring in the last men and supplies in the more unwieldy boats.

Turner was obdurate—and then Smith became more so. He managed to discover that Betio was virtually encircled by a protective screen—two screens—of barbed wire, and a series of concrete obstacles. Turner was assuming that the landing boats could come in over the reef. If not, said Smith, they were in trouble. He insisted on his amtracs. When Turner still said no, Smith played his final card.

If there were no amtracs, he would not go.

Only then did Kelly Turner back down and let "Howling Mad" Smith have his way.

D-Day was to be November 20, 1943. On that much they could all agree. It should be a little easier because on November 1, the Americans were also planning to invade Bougainville, the largest of the Solomon Islands. That operation ought to tie down much of the Japanese fleet and most of Japan's air power.

Because of this, Admiral Montgomery was to take the *Essex,* the *Bunker Hill,* and the *Independence* and Admiral Sherman was to take the *Saratoga* and the *Princeton* down to the south to support Halsey, and then hurry back in time for the Gilberts operation.

Two groups—three escort carriers each—were to support the marines ashore with tactical air power. Admiral Ragsdale commanded one of these, and Admiral Mullinix the other.

And in spite of all Towers' requests, complaints, and anguished cries, the big carriers were not to be allowed to go into the Marshalls and strike at Japanese air bases to knock out the enemy's air power before the fight began.

This was a very sore point indeed, and Towers and his junior admirals and captains were upset about it. They were right in their thinking; later it would be revealed that Montgomery and Sherman, who had struck hard at Rabaul several times early in November in support of the Bougainville operation, had hit so very hard that the Japanese were unable when the time came to send any air assistance to the Gilberts. Had the airmen been able to hit the Marshalls in the same way, they might have saved a good deal of trouble and some lives.

While the Americans were scurrying about, ready to launch their invasion, the Japanese were not idle. The small boats continued to move. The workers contined to pour concrete and strengthen the defenses with coconut logs and even steel reinforcing rods.

The decision had been made in the cold reality of summer: the Gilberts would not be basically reinforced. The garrison there was going to have to stick it out alone, with every man dedicated to defense to the last, if it came to that.

Captain Sugano knew that, and so did his officers. They had been told, long before, that their lives belonged to the emperor and the glory of Nippon.

In October, the Japanese high command forecast an attack soon on the Gilberts. They did not expect it within a matter of days, however, because in the Bougainville battle, the Japanese commanders had mistakenly sent back word that they had inflicted serious defeat on the American carrier forces.

There was, also, a strong segment of opinion at Truk and in Tokyo the Gilberts would not be attacked at all, but that the Americans would move directly to the Marshalls.

Since the Marshalls were an important line of defense, and the Gilberts far less so, Japanese strength was concentrated in the

Marshalls, and the Gilberts continued to be neglected.

Admiral Koga, the chief of the Combined Fleet, had reassessed the strategic situation at Truk in the summer, and had been forced to carry out the gloomy predictions of Admiral Yamamoto of times past. The balance had changed with Guadalcanal in American hands. So Koga set out to limit the strategic defense positions, and he drew two circles, one within the other. The first, or primary, circle included the natural-resources areas, the Marianas, and the Carolines. But the larger circle where the Marshalls, Gilberts, Solomons, and New Guinea fell was to be defended with what existed, and what might be spared. No major effort would be made.

There was one possible exception: Koga and his admirals kept watching for the opportunity to stage the "decisive sea battle" in which the Japanese fleet would sail forth and demolish the American fleet.

That was the Japanese dream at this stage of the war—only by some such miraculous occurrence could they win the struggle, and the high command knew it.

To keep track of the American effort, the Japanese had to rely more and more on submarine surveillance as their air power was whittled down by the Americans in the South Pacific.

The submarine *I-35* was to play a role in these operations, and in the battle for the Gilberts. She was under the command of Lieutenant Commander Takeo Yamamoto, and she was to head into American waters very soon.

I-35 was manned by nine officers and eighty-one men. Lieutenant Abe was the executive officer, Lieutenant Yamasaki the chief engineer, and Lieutenant Hari the navigator. The doctor was Lieutenant (J.G.) Kamura.

These officers were virtually unknown to the men, except in their divisions. The captain was known to them all, for while the average age of the submarine's crew was twenty-five, he was nearly forty years old, and was regarded by his men as a "father," from Superior Petty Officer Ichiro Yamashita, a farm boy from the country, to Takashi Kawano, a city boy whose family owned a small toymaking business. Kawano served as a messenger in the control room.

Morale was high, there was plenty of fresh food, they had radios and could receive Tokyo. They had beer and sake available, vitamin pills, and grape sugar for injections. They had been at sea for as long as fifty-six days at a stretch without a man reporting sick.

So when Admiral Koga ordered that she head from Truk for Samoa and the Fiji area to scout out any possible American intentions there, the crew and captain were ready. On October 11, I-35 sailed.

But when they were near Canton island, I-35 had a change in orders. She was to head for the Hawaiian islands and patrol about 100 miles southeast of Pearl Harbor. Specifically, she was to look for an invasion fleet that was reported to be heading for Wake Island. (This was the immediate Japanese reaction to the raids on Wake that month.)

Lieutenant Commander Yamamoto told Lieutenant Hari to set the proper course, and on October 23, I-35 arrived on station and began a twenty-three-day patrol there. She knew one other submarine was in the area, and she watched for this friend. Otherwise all she would see would be enemies.

Nearly all the day, I-35 stayed down at about 60 feet, coming up three or four times every hour to periscope depth for a look around. She ranged back and forth from 50 to 300 miles out, covering the wide angle where a fleet might be found outward bound, heading for Wake.

One day Yamamoto did undertake an attack, although this was not his mission. He fired three torpedoes at a 7,000-ton merchant ship off Pearl Harbor. But he had miscalculated the speed of the merchant ship, and all the torpedoes missed.

On another occasion, I-35 was attacked. The men heard the noises of propellers coming toward them fast. The ship came on, and dropped four depth charges, but not one of them was closer than 500 yards away, and they did no damage. Yamamoto took her down to 160 feet, and stayed there for a time. But the destroyer seemed to lose interest rapidly and went away. *I-35* went about her business.

By November 15 she had seen nothing. Yamamoto had new orders that day: when he surfaced after dark to communicate with Truk he was told to head for Espiritu Santo and then to investigate any activity in the Fijis.

The invasion force was already assembling. It was difficult for the Japanese to comprehend what was happening, because the ships were coming from so many directions.

Admiral Harry Hill had flown to Auckland and joined General Julian Smith, commander of the Second Marine Division. They came north, leaving on November 1 in the transports, to rendezvous with Hill's naval force at Efate in the New Hebrides. By November 13, they had arrived, held a practice invasion there, and sailed for Tarawa.

The carriers lent to Halsey refueled and headed for the Gilberts on November 14. Off the Gilberts they would rendezvous with Admiral Pownall's force, which had sailed from Pearl Harbor on November 10, unnoticed by *I-35*. So did the Northern Attack Force, accompanied by Admiral Spruance. So ships were coming from Pearl Harbor, Efate, Samoa, Funafuti, and San Diego, to converge on the Gilberts for D-Day, November 20.

Spruance's flagship was the twelve-year-old cruiser *Indianapolis*. The ship really was not adequate for the task, for its accommodations for an admiral and his staff were extremely limited. The admiral's quarters had been planned for half a dozen. Spruance brought a staff of thirty-two aboard with him.

There was a standup desk for the admiral, and charts to show the location of the Fifth Fleet ships and the enemy, and these were watched day and night by young plotting officers. At any moment the admiral could look at the chart and have the latest intelligence available about the course of operations.

When Spruance went aboard the *Indianapolis* there came complications: Admiral Halsey's borrowed carriers, cruisers, and destroyers. Spruance worried that they would not be back in time for his operation (never, if they were sunk down south), and so the Gilberts movement was delayed for twenty-four hours. And Spruance made an alternative plan: if the ships did not get back, they would hit Tarawa, and when that was taken, move on to Makin.

On November 8, the cruiser *Birmingham,* one of those lent out, had been torpedoed and badly damaged. She was out of action for Operation Galvanic, and Spruance and his staff were shaken by the loss.

He made arrangements with Nimitz to send a message that would tell him, even at sea, which of the two plans of operations were to be put into effect.

That was the best he could do, so the *Indianapolis* sailed, along with a number of other ships. Some would join them en route, some at their destination. Some would go from other ports directly to their assigned positions. It was not a case of a long train of ships setting out from one place, but an assemblage of vessels to meet at a certain time, in certain places, and undertake certain actions. In that sense, it was the best security possible; the Japanese could have no indication of a huge invasion force setting out from one place, when the Tarawa invaders, for example, were coming up from the South Pacific.

The *Indianapolis* steamed with Turner's force that would attack Makin, and when they neared the equator the ships became so hot that in the interior cabins temperatures rose to over 100 degrees.

On November 13, Spruance was relieved to know that all the other ships Halsey had borrowed had been returned, and the first plan for the Gilberts would go into effect.

Admiral John Hoover's land-based aircraft from the Ellice Islands began their air strikes that day, bombing, strafing, and taking pictures of the Gilberts and Marshalls. The islands seemed quiet enough. It never did seem that it would be a difficult task with all this force.

Spruance knew, though, that if there was going to be trouble it would probably come at Tarawa, so on November 18, when the Tarawa force came up from the south and met the Makin force, the *Indianapolis* joined Admiral Hill's ships.

He and Hill exchanged notes about plans. They agreed that it was imperative that they get the troops ashore and consolidate the occupation of Tarawa very quickly, before the enemy could react.

On the night before the battle, Spruance watched the movie in the wardroom, and after it was over, he went to bed, uncommunicative as ever.

In the air strikes on the Gilberts and Marshalls that began on November 13, B-24s manned by army air force troops hit first. The carriers were still not allowed to cut loose.

The Japanese plan for defense of the Gilberts and Marshalls (for by now the headquarters at Truk was expecting attack) had called for use of the Second Fleet from Truk and the dispatch of long-range planes from the Bismarcks and short-range planes from Truk, plus ships of the fleet to sail and fight.

At the end of the second week of November, however, Admiral Koga and Admiral Kondo, commander of the Second Fleet, were in no position to carry out such plans. The Second Fleet's cruisers had been so badly mauled at Rabaul in the carrier-plane attack of November 5 that they could not be used. Further, the stepped-up campaign in the western Solomons committed all the short-range planes at Truk. There was nothing much to send, and so nothing much was sent.

The Japanese garrisons in the islands around the Gilberts were alerted, by flyovers, by attacks, by a sense of urgency that told them something important was afoot.

At Mili, the Japanese had a relatively strong force, largely to service aircraft that would pass along this island-hopping route, which at this time in the war extended from the Solomons all the way back to Japan.

Captain Masanari Shiga was the senior officer of Mili. His executive officer was Lieutenant Commander Hiroshi Tokuno. They expected attack, and they had some 2,000 men to defend the place. There were also two air units, consisting of about 500 officers and men, including pilots.

Then, on November 15, the first attack came.

Ten B-24s appeared over Mili, and bombed. When they left, Captain Shiga counted his casualities: ten dead, ten wounded, two barracks burned, and the bomb-fuse warehouse destroyed. It could have been worse.

Next day came another raid, but this was from high altitude, and accomplished nothing. No casualties, no damage. On November 18, nineteen B-24s flew over, and again did little damage. Next day another ten came, and still no damage.

During these raids the Nakajima 97 bombers (Bettys) took off and fled the fields, so that they would not be destroyed on the ground. One or two of them tried to intercept the B-24s, but they were not built for such fighting, and they accomplished nothing. One Betty was caught on the ground in a raid, but luckily escaped without damage.

Then came November 19—D – 1 Day.

At Truk, Commander Goro Matsuura was waiting to go into action. Previous instructions had indicated that when an attack came on the Marshalls or Gilberts his Flotilla 22 was to be ready.

But although Commander Matsuura was moved up to the Marshalls, the planes were not. Altogether they had forty bombers, thirty fighters, and five flying boats to defend the area against the American attackers, plus the eighteen dive bombers at Mili.

At Tokyo, when the signal of attack was raised the naval air authorities made an attempt to reinforce, and send Air Flotilla 24 —forty bombers and thirty fighters—from Hokkaido and the Kuriles. Another eighteen fighters were moved from Rabaul, although they could hardly be spared.

The whole operation was an indication of the Japanese weakness in numerical strength and equipment in the face of the Americans with their hundreds of carrier planes, plus hundreds more shore-based naval planes and army bombers and fighters.

As the carrier and land-based bomber raids continued in November, the Japanese made last-minute plans. From the Marshalls they put out scout planes, four a day, in an effort to secure as much advance warning as they could.

When the time came, they proposed to attack at dawn with

fighters and bombers, and to drive off the enemy forces.

On November 16 one scout at Wotje was ordered to fly to Nauru, and work that area. At 3:00 on the morning of November 19 Lieutenant Kioki Yoshoyo sighted what he thought was the American fleet. In fact, it was only part of the fleet, part of those 200 ships that were coming to invade the Gilberts.

Excitedly the pilot radioed Kwajalein, the headquarters of the Marshalls: Enemy contact. Fleet sighted. Several carriers and other types too numerous to mention.

Kwajalein gave orders: attack. So eight torpedo planes set out to attack the Americans. Meanwhile, the U.S. forces hit Nauru, and damaged two fighters and three bombers on the ground. The slender Japanese air force was becoming even slenderer still.

That day, the 19th, and on the 20th, the Japanese began to have a better picture of what was occurring. Several other scout planes saw elements of the fleet. They could not make much of what they saw: what was the meaning of four cargo ships steaming at 20 knots toward Tarawa?

At sea, Lieutenant Commander Yamamoto had new orders, radioed to him by Truk even as he was heading for Fiji. He was to abandon that mission and head now for Tarawa, for headquarters suspected the invasion was coming at the Gilberts. He was to attack American shipping and sink warships and transports. There would be half a dozen other Japanese submarines in the vicinity to undertake the same task.

6
INVASION

Marine Colonel Merritt A. Edson was under no illusions about the job ahead for the marines on Tarawa. It was true that Carlson's raiders had not found much activity in the Gilberts a year earlier, but that was meaningless. Here, now, was another "raider," for Edson had commanded the First Raider Battalion which had saved the airfield at Guadalcanal from capture in September. Edson knew where he had been, where he was going, and how difficult it was likely to be.

The call for "hazardous duty in the south" was issued not only in the various outposts of Japan's empire in 1942, it was also posted in the various naval barracks and headquarters in the home islands.

For after Carlson's Makin raid, the Japanese were worried about the Gilberts. Carlson and his men had killed the garrison on Makin, and they had destroyed the seaplane base the naval authorities had put there.

Obviously, if the Gilberts were to be valuable they would have to be heavily fortified.

And so Rear Admiral Saichiro was selected to command the whole rebuilding of Gilberts' defenses, at Betio, where the British had maintained their colonial outpost until that day in December 1941 when a Japanese occupation force had taken over, and at Makin in the north, which was also fortified. So was tiny Abemama in the far south.

Saichiro nearly completed the work, and then he was relieved by a stocky admiral of quite a different sort. Saichiro had been the naval constructor, an engineer. But Rear Admiral Keiji Shibasaki was a fighting officer, and that was why he was sent to the Gilberts, to defend the place against invasion.

Among those who had answered the call for "hazardous duty in the south" was a young petty officer, Tadeo Oonuki, a small-town boy from Kasumigaura. Petty Officer Oonuki had served for several years, and served well to achieve his rank. He had been to China and to Indochina. But his duties had been shore duties almost entirely, and while his friends fought in the battles of the ships and came back with tales of glory, Tadeo Oonuki spent most of his time driving a truck and picking up supplies.

Assigned to Yokosuka Naval Base in the spring of 1943, he saw the call for volunteers and decided it was a way to get some excitement out of the war.

With others who volunteered, he was shipped to Tarawa aboard a cruiser in July, and there they were processed into the special landing force. Petty Officer Oonuki's skill as a truck driver got him a job driving at Type 97 tank, which was armed with a 37mm gun and two 7.7mm machine guns. His assignment in case of attack was to protect Admiral Shibasaki's command post.

Like Ensign Oka and the others, Petty Officer Oonuki settled into the routine. The duties were light enough, and there was plenty of time for swimming. In the evenings, he joined others to drink sake and tell stories. He soon made friends with Torpedo Officer Yoshio Tanikaze, who ran one of Ensign Oka's boats. They got together almost every night to smoke and drink sake until their faces grew red, and the stories funnier. They listened to the radio, to Tokyo for the most part.

Occasionally big four-engined American bombers came over

to drop bombs, but they dropped from high altitude and did not hurt much of anything.

On the morning of November 19, as noted, while on a flight out of the Marshalls, Lieutenant Yoshoyo had spotted the American fleet.

And so at Truk, Admiral Koga knew: the Americans were going to strike the Gilberts.

On Betio, Admiral Shibasaki had the word that day, and he issued his orders. The men of the Imperial Japanese Navy were to defend their positions to the last man. It was time to go to their battle stations.

They had been trained and exhorted in the tradition of bushido. They did not think of survival, but of dying honorably for the emperor, and taking with them as many of the enemy as possible. Then, after death, their souls would assemble at the Yasukuni shrine, that holiest of places for the warriors of Japan, and they would have eternal rest and eternal glory.

They were ready.

On the ground, the alarm was sounded when the American planes were sighted. Ensign Oka went to his designated pillbox. The others went where they were assigned, and they waited.

Petty Officer Oonuki's post in an air raid was inside the shelter of the command-post blockhouse, but in various drills he had gone in there and he did not care for it. There were just too many people, the smell of stale sweat and sake and cigarettes was overwhelming, and he had long since decided that the best place for him in a raid was inside his tank.

So that is where he went when the alarm rang. He was not so certain it had been a good idea when the American planes came in low and strafed. He could hear the bullets ricocheting; he waited, wondering if he would come out of it alive.

Torpedo Officer Tanikaze was out on routine patrol around the lagoon that day when the planes came in from the east. He was a sitting duck. He turned the boat toward Eita, down the chain of islets from Betio, and tried to make the safety of the beach. But a Hellcat swooped in on him, firing .50-caliber bullets that plunked like stones into the water alongside the boat. The plane climbed, swung around in a quick turn, and came back. This time the pilot's aim was more certain—the bullets smashed into the boat. The crewmen leaped over the side as the craft began to sink, and struck out, swimming, for the safety of shore. Tanikaze never made it; the Hellcat gunned him in the water, and he slipped below the surface.

That night, the men of the garrison turned toward Tokyo and recited the Imperial Rescript to Soldiers and Sailors that reminded them of their oaths to live, to fight, to die, perhaps, for the Emperor and the glory of Nippon. The men were unusually silent, thinking of Torpedo Officer Tanikaze and the other nineteen who had been killed in the raid.

Next day, Admiral Shibasaki radioed Japan. The Americans were obviously getting ready to attack the Gilberts, he reported. He needed more supplies—more cement to strengthen the blockhouses and make new defenses.

Ensign Oka, Petty Officer Oonuki, and the rest were put to work harder than ever. The blockhouses and pillboxes were increased in numbers and strength; 5-foot concrete walls were not uncommon. And they were covered with sand until they looked like nothing more than big anthills. The blockhouses and pillboxes were armed with 75mm, 70mm, and 37mm guns, and scores of machine guns that were sighted in to manage overlapping fields of fire. Between them were dug the trenches with foxholes planned on a spiderweb pattern, the slit trenches panning out from the central core.

What Admiral Shibasaki had ended up with then, after all the efforts of Ensign Ota, Petty Officer Oonuki, and the rest, was a veritable fortress.

The invaders, if not the defenders, thought of Betio as a bird, with the beak pointing up toward the lagoon, the breast divided by the long pier, then the tail tapering off to point directly toward Bairiki, the next islet in the twisting chain that was the Tarawa atoll.

Betio was 2 miles long and 500 yards wide at its widest point, which meant that at no place would an enemy be immune from fire. The airfield had a strip 4,000 feet long, with several taxiways, and most of the rest of the land was covered by coconut palms. From the air it seemed tranquil, scarcely defended. But on the ground, as the Americans were to discover after the battle, Betio in the first days of November was one of the most heavily defended areas for its size on the face of the earth.

For the Japanese had used terrain, coral, barbed wire, concrete, coconut logs, coral sand, armor plate, and every other material at their disposal to make the island invasion-proof. They had studied fields of fire, and overlapped their gun positions so that two guns fired on almost every inch of territory. They had brought in British Vickers naval guns, captured at Singapore, ranging from 5 inches to 8 inches in the bore.

The pillboxes, armored revetments, blockhouses, and bomb-proof shelters were all designed so that they could be used against a landing force from either side of the island, from the sea or from the lagoon.

As the moment of invasion approached, many reports came back to Admiral Spruance and to the marines. The army airmen announced that on their last bombing of Betio they had seen no signs of life, and only the weakest of antiaircraft fire. Perhaps, some hoped, the Japanese were pulling out of Tarawa just as they had pulled out of Kiska in the Aleutians. When the Americans and Canadians had landed on Kiska there was not a Japanese to be found.

This optimistic frame of mind seemed to increase among the officers of the Second Marine Division as they neared the islands.

As for the Japanese on Tarawa and Makin, they expected air and sea reinforcement if and when an attack commenced. But two days before the actual landings, the communications system had already been destroyed and several planes on Betio knocked out, and the Japanese defenders were quite alone, with no way of calling for help.

The only radio set left in working condition on the island was the emergency set in the admiral's command post. And that was not to be used except at the very end.

The submarine U.S.S. *Nautilus* was an old hand in these waters. She had carried Carlson's raiders on that mission more than a year before, and on the 18th she was off Tarawa observing the weather, surf, landing hazards, and the results of bombardments.

Then she was to move on to deliver some marines to Abemama.

That night, having corrected some errors in the plans by pointing out compass mistakes in the mapping, the *Nautilus* was getting ready to move out. At 11:00, she was going. Just then, the destroyer *Ringgold* picked up a signal on the radar, moving south at 20 knots. Hill gave the order:

Fire.

The *Ringgold*'s first salvo hit the *Nautilus* at the base of the conning tower, rupturing her main induction valve, and letting in 30 tons of water—in other words, very nearly sinking her.

Commander W. D. Irvin took her down, and managed to avoid his friends. It was the narrowest escape she had during the operation.

On Betio the bombardment grew so fierce on the afternoon of November 19 that Ensign Ota, the small-boat commander, finally gave up all hope of maintaining his command on the shore and retreated within a six-man concrete pillbox. There was no communication with the captain, or any other group on Betio, except by runner, and during the daylight hours the runner was likely to be blown up by a bomb or strafed by a plane if a pilot spotted him moving across an open spot.

But the pillbox was secure enough. There had been several hits by shellfire, and more hits by bombs during the hours before the assault began. The pillbox was sound and undamaged.

Unfortunately not all the pillboxes on Betio, even the big ones, had been converted to concrete. So some of the American bombs and shells did do damage—three of the pillboxes were knocked out in those early hours of the fighting, before the Japanese had even seen the faces of their enemies.

What surprised Ensign Ota about the whole thing, as he sat in the pillbox on the night of November 19, was the suddenness and the fury of it all. The Japanese on Betio had no warning, not one bit, from a higher headquarters, and then suddenly the storm had been unleashed on them, and when they awakened on the morning of the 20th, there outside was a huge fleet of ships and transports about which they had been told nothing whatsoever.

In that early-morning bombardment on Tarawa, there was damage. For 800 of the defenders were assigned the area of the beaches.

The marines aboard the transports were out of bed at midnight, and in the first moments of November 20, sweating, straining, and swearing, they were heading for chow. The night was almost inhumanly hot, and the ships hotter, closed down for the blackout as they had to be.

The call to general quarters came at 2:15 aboard the transport on which *Life* correspondent Robert Sherrod was riding.

Just after 5:00 in the morning, the big ships began their plastering of the island, as Ensign Ota sat in his pillbox and Correspondent Sherrod roamed the decks of the transport, in his fatigues, with his camouflage helmet on his head, and in it a sheaf of toilet paper and a mosquito headnet, while he mingled with the marines who were waiting.

Intelligence reports assembled for the attack on Tarawa indicated that the Japanese had eight coastal guns, six small coastal guns, four heavy antiaircraft guns, twenty-four light guns, and sixty-eight beach and antiboat guns. But the aerial photographs had been fooled by the Japanese camouflage and the job done by those construction men, who hid the guns cleverly in emplacements of coconut logs and reinforced concrete.

But as the Southern Attack Force moved in to the landing area, there was no sound from the shore guns. They arrived at a point about 8 miles off Betio island, and the landing craft began assembling for the first assault wave. It would be dawn just before 5:00, and it was time to get going.

Already, the ships were encountering difficulty: the currents were stronger than anyone had expected and the transports drifted out of position as they waited to unload.

Before long, the Japanese fired red starshells. They knew the enemy had come.

For nearly half an hour nothing happened. Clouds broke, and the sky became clearer minute by minute. But Betio was there, silent. Those who thought Betio might have been evacuated had already been proved wrong. The starshells showed that there were Japanese on the island. But how many? That no one knew.

On the night of November 19, the task group was just out of sight of the atoll, and the ships crept in quietly in the gathering darkness. From the *Maryland,* Admiral Hill could see the lights of the island, still turned on, when the *Maryland* came into sight of Betio at 2:50.

Five minutes later, Transport Commander Knowles reported to Admiral Hill that the sixteen transports were in position. The sound of bosun's pipes could be heard across the water, and then the whine of electric winches as the landing boats were let into the water and began to circle the troopships.

A red light on the leading cruiser was blinking, and then the lights of Betio went out, and a powerful searchlight flashed from the northwest corner of the island, and began sweeping across the horizon. It found a transport, lingered there, and then went out.

The silence was eerie in the blackness.

At 3:30 the alarm rang throughout the flagship: general quarters. The show was about to begin.

From the shore of Betio, there was nothing to see now in the darkness. Petty Officer Oonuki sat inside his Type 97 tank, parked beside the admiral's blockhouse headquarters.

At 4:41, Lieutenant Commander E.A. MacPherson was catapulted off the flagship in his float plane; his would be the task of spotting for the bombardment that was to be unleashed by the battleships, cruisers, and destroyers in a few minutes.

From the shore, the catapult launcher made a bright-red flash alongside the *Maryland,* and in a moment, from the northwest blockhouse, one of the big shore guns fired an 8-inch shell that splashed a few hundred feet beyond the *Maryland.*

The battleships and cruisers swung around, and one of the battleships let go a salvo that screamed over the heads of the marines in their landing boats and splashed into the lagoon.

On the flagship, Captain Ryan stood on his bridge, with Admiral Hill alongside.

"Shall we go ahead, sir?" the captain asked.

"Yes," said the admiral.

The captain turned to the TBS.

"Commence firing," he told the ships. "The war is on."

"Stand by for main battery," came the squawk over the *Maryland*'s speaker system. Then there was a warning buzz, and the after four 16-inch guns fired.

The ship flinched as if struck, and quivered, and dust began to fall down from hidden corners on high. Several lights were knocked out, and the radio set went on the blink.

And then the forward turrets fired, and then the after turrets again. The din became unimaginable, repeated on every warship in the fleet, with all the projectiles aimed for that one little island.

Almost immediately a shell found an ammunition dump in the grassy triangle in the center of Betio. The whole island's center seemed to go up in flame; the palms were illuminated and their shadows stood black against the sands below.

Then the firing stopped.

There was a reason for it: Admiral Hill had learned belatedly that the troopships were in the wrong place; they hampered the warships' field of fire, and they were within range of the Japanese shore guns. They had to be gotten out of there, fast.

The airmen had said that given the chance they would knock out all the Japanese installations from the air. Edson knew better.

The battleship men said they would clean the beaches with their big guns. Edson knew better than that, too.

He told Robert Sherrod that he expected a very tough fight for Tarawa. Some of his battalion commanders thought it might all be over in three hours. But Edson, as chief of staff, and General Julian Smith knew better. They knew their Japanese soldiers and sailors.

In the gathering light, the Japanese opened fire with the 8-inch guns they had brought in from the Singapore defenses after the Makin raid. The guns began to fire, sporadically, aimed at the expeditionary force in general.

So there were heavy guns on the island. They had not been knocked out by the previous gunfire, or by the air bombardment of recent days.

Admiral Harry Hill's flagship, the *Maryland,* began to open fire on the enemy. The *Maryland* fired ten salvos from her big 16-inch guns. On the fifth salvo her gunnery officer reported a hit on the shore battery that had been firing. There was an explosion. The Japanese gun did stop. And then the other ships of the support force began to fire on the shore, and the din became terrific, the smoke rose up with gouts of sand and the ripped trunks of palms as the guns searched the island for Japanese emplacements.

It was a large bang in a small place. Betio was only 2¼ miles long and half a mile wide. Or, to put it more in civilian terms, it was a little more than a third the size of New York City's Central Park.

For half an hour the ships' guns blasted red and yellow flames through the gathering light, and the shore was silent. Then the ships stopped firing.

The Japanese opened up again, stronger than ever.

All this while, the marines were still getting into the assault boats, which then milled about, staying on the move and trying to keep out of the way of the shore fire. The curtain of smoke that the ships' shelling had put up over the island still hung there, drifting lazily. Fires started here and there burned brightly for a time, and then lowered.

The American planes came in then, scores of dive bombers, coming down screaming, torpedo bombers, coming in on a gentle slant to loose their bombs, and fighters, zooming in over the island with .50-caliber machine guns spitting tracer bullets that kicked up spurts of sand and dirt.

The Japanese were firing on the transports now, and some of the shells came close enough to make the men realize that it was going to get rougher before the day was over. One shell burst 20 feet from the bow of the transport *LaSalle,* denting the ship's plating and spraying the decks with water. That was too close for comfort.

LST-34, which had been loaded with amphibious landing vehicles, was very nearly hit. Her crew watched as the Japanese gunners began to find the range.

A salvo struck 700 years off the port bow.

Another came in, 300 yards off the port beam.

The third salvo splashes were 100 yards off the starboard quarter.

The fourth salvo was only 30 yards astern.

With that one, at 6:15, in the daylight, *LST-34* put on full speed and zigzagged away.

The Japanese were coming too close. The transports turned and got out of there, and the assault craft in the water came right after them.

They went back until they were 10 miles off the beach. Before they could get out of the way, two men aboard the transport *Harris* were injured by shellfire and one man on the *William P. Biddle* was hit.

The Japanese had drawn blood.

As if infuriated, the warships opened up again on the shore batteries, and as they did so, the Japanese quit firing. It was impossible to tell if the guns had been destroyed or if the gunners were sitting there, waiting.

The transports continued then to unload their assault waves

into the little boats that would move on the schedule so precisely worked out at Pearl Harbor in the last few weeks.

The assault waves then began to move in, heading for Beaches Red One, Red Two, and Red Three.

The landings would be made in the lagoon, and to accomplish them a minesweeper led the way toward the passage through the reef.

U.S.S. *Pursuit* led the way, followed by U.S.S. *Requisite,* while LCVPs (landing craft, vehicles, personnel) laid smoke pots between there and shore to screen the move from the enemy.

Just outside the entrance to the lagoon, the destroyers *Ringgold* and *Dashiell* waited. And when the shore batteries opened up on the minesweepers in spite of the smoke, the destroyers began firing on them, causing the Japanese gunners to stop shooting.

When the channel was swept, the *Pursuit* began marking the assault lanes so that the landing craft would have a clear shot at the beaches. The *Requisite* went back to pick up the destroyers and lead them through into the lagoon.

The Japanese gunners opened up again. A shell struck the *Ringgold* aft, and went through her thin metal plating, but did not explode. Another glanced off a torpedo tube, failed to explode, and ended up in the emergency radio room.

The destroyers spotted the position and began to fire. In a moment there was a tremendous explosion ashore. A shell had apparently struck an ammunition dump.

At 7:15, while the *Ringgold* fought the Japanese shore batteries, the *Pursuit* switched on her searchlight to guide the LVTs in through the channel. It was necessary to pierce the waves of dust and smoke that covered the area like a gray blanket.

The *Pursuit* had been tracking the landing craft on radar. Now she reported to Admiral Hill that the assault was twenty-four minutes behind schedule. That caused the first postponement of the landing.

Aboard the flagship, the radios were acting up. The old battleship had been roughly treated to put in the communications for a major command vessel. And she objected; now as her big guns fired, the radios went on and off. That added to the confusion;

it prevented the flagship from making contact with the air units, to change the signals on the air strikes.

So the planes, which should have been delayed until the last moment so they could deliver maximum shock value just before the troops made the shore, came in and strafed the beaches of Betio. The *Maryland* had to shut down her big guns in order to use the radio and call off the air strike.

The firing went on then, until 9:00, the new time for the landings of H-hour.

Colonel Shoup, who was leading the landing forces in, had decided to send Major Henry P. Crowe's Second Battalion of the Eighth Marine Regiment in to storm Beach Red Three, which lay east of the long pier that jutted out into the lagoon.

On his right would be Lieutenant Colonel Herbert Amey's Second Battalion, Second Marines, on Red Beach Two, and on the far right Major John F. Schoettel, Third Battalion, Second Marines, would land on Beach Red One, a crescent-shaped beach that was 500 yards wide.

In the morning when the guns began to fire, Admiral Spruance could see nothing, because the *Indianapolis* had been sent around the corner of the island to engage in an independent firing mission as part of the bombardment. He listened to the radio, caught samples of the action, and saw enough in clouds of smoke to feel that the bombardment was very effective.

Just after 6:00 in the morning he saw the carrier planes come in from Admiral Montgomery's carriers.

The planes flew over, bombed and strafed, and then moved off. Spruance was not conscious of the difficulties, of the wrong timing, of the errors, of the difficulties that dogged every step.

He saw the first wave of marines go in, in the amphibious tractors, but much of the scene was veiled in the smoke that hung over the island.

On the flag bridge of the *Maryland,* Admiral Hill, General Julian Smith, and Colonel Edson waited and watched through their glasses. They saw the little boats and amtracs circling around.

"They'll go in standing up," somebody shouted. "There aren't fifty Japs left alive on that island."

The naval gunfire, everyone believed, had done its job.

But then as the boats approached the beaches, from the bridge the commanders could see that there was trouble. In the water, a long, long way from shore, the boats began to stop, apparently without reason. Then the little green-clad figures began to jump out and start to wade in.

"At that distance they seemed hardly to be moving at all," said Lieutenant Commander Kenneth McArdle, a fleet public-relations officer. "They would be waist-deep now, and suddenly just their heads would be sticking out, and their arms with rifles clutched high over head. Now and then one would slip down into the water and not appear again. . . ."

That was not at all the way the planners had planned it.

The foulup of the bombardment and the air strikes had created new difficulties, because, of course, the plan had been drawn with a view to the tidal conditions. The planners had wanted to get the troops ashore at high tide so that they would have the full advantage of deep water over the reef until they got into the beach.

Already, judging by the delay, there was difficulty to be expected about that.

One of the boat officers guiding the first amtracs saw it first: they came in to within 800 yards from the beach, almost a third of a mile out, and the coral reef showed, with 3 feet of water over it. For the amtracs that was all right. They were designed to move on sea or land.

But it was not going to be all right for the landing craft.

Someone had blundered.

Captain Moore watched all this with Spruance aboard the *Indianapolis*. They saw the fires burning everywhere, the coconut trees blasted and burning, and the troops coming in. It seemed that it would be a simple operation for them to take control.

Then they saw the LVTs ground on the reef, far offshore. And they knew that was not part of the plan.

The waves of amphibious tractors came in, and they came raggedly.

The Japanese began firing shrapnel, but it had little effect at long range. Neither did the machine-gun fire seem to matter much just then.

First in was the Second Scout sniper platoon of Lieutenant William D. Hawkins. It came in at the end of the pier, up onto the pier, and over a pile of gasoline drums the Japanese had stashed there to impede progress. The bullets began twanging off the drums as they came. Hawkins took four scouts and a man with a flamethrower, and advanced. They knocked out two little shacks that were apparently harboring machine guns, and the flames burned through the pier itself. The others began coming in.

At 8:55 the guns stopped firing. It was five minutes from landing time. Dust and smoke screened the island from the ships offshore, and the planes came in overhead and shot up the beaches.

Major Schoettel's troops landed on Red One at ten minutes after H-Hour. They came to Red One, climbed over the 4-foot log barricade, and moved inland. The Japanese fire was severe. The Japanese had a strongpoint between Red One and Red Two, and it was going to give the marines much trouble in the next hour. A hundred men would die in its shadow.

The battalion mortar platoon found its LCVPs grounded 500 yards offshore and had to wade in. It suffered 35 percent casualties on the way.

Then in came Major Crowe's battalion, in onto Red Three, and most of the men stopped just at the end of the barricades.

Toughest of all was Lieutenant Colonel Amey's landing on Red Two. One platoon was driven off the proper landing place by boat-gun fire, and had to land on Red One. The rest were pinned down quickly, and managed to get only a foothold of 50 yards on the beach.

As the marines came, the Japanese proved that they were not dead, nor were they asleep. They opened up again with the big guns on the transports.

In the amphibious vehicles the marines crouched low. Some of them swore. Some of them shivered with the chill wind that swept along inside the craft, and some of them sat, half stunned, waiting.

Over their heads the firing was going again, back and forth. Those who could rise up to see the flat island ahead could see flames and smoke again. It seemed hard to believe that anything could be living on that island after the pasting it had taken from air and sea bombardment. And yet the Japanese guns continued to fire.

Correspondent Sherrod, moving onto Red Three, crouched in his landing amtrac, looked up, and counted ninety-two planes over the island at one time. The fires were roaring, and occasionally something exploded with a spectacular spout of wreathing smoke and flickering flame. Ammunition dump? Fuel dump? Whatever it was it heartened the men who saw, for it meant the enemy was deprived of one bit more of his dreadful capacity to kill them.

It was not obvious to the men in the little boats, but it was now obvious to their leaders back on the big ships that something had already gone wrong with the timing. The assault had been supposed to hit the beaches at a little after 8:00. It was actually 9:10 when they made the beaches, and the boats could not clear the reef. That meant the men had to be shifted into the amtracs, which meant more time in the water, more time as sitting ducks for the Japanese to pot at with whatever guns they had.

On the beaches, the Japanese—some 800 of them—were greeting the marines with rifle, machine-gun, and heavier-gun fire as they came ashore. Marines were falling and dying.

The Japanese had not been responsible for the first major American casualties; they came from accident. A turret aboard the old battleship *Mississippi* blew up, killing forty-three men and wounding nineteen others.

During the first lull in the bombardment when the troopships were moving, Admiral Shibasaki moved his troops about, using the telephonic communications that had been set up all through the island. Petty Officer Oonuki's tank was released from its bondage at headquarters, and he was instructed to find a place to fire on the lagoon beaches. It was obvious that the landings would be carried out here.

So Oonuki found a spot halfway between the revetments of the airfield and the cover into which the invaders would come. He watched as the boats and the amphibious tractors came in, and the boats stopped on the reef, and the small green buglike figures wriggled out and began swimming and wading ashore. Oonuki manned his 7.7mm machine gun and began firing on the approaching men in the water. He saw some of them fall, and he kept on firing.

He saw two American tanks coming toward the beach, and he was in a quandary: should he go down and meet them for a tank fight?

He heard some thumping on the side of the tank, and he peered through the narrow vision slot. A sailor was there banging on the tank with his rifle. They made communication, finally, and the sailor told him he was to move the tank back to the admiral's headquarters immediately.

The decision was made for him. He wheeled the tank around and headed back to the blockhouse, the sailor running alongside, away from the ships and the sea.

On the 19th, the submarine *Plunger* had come to a point a few miles off Mili atoll. In fact she had been lurking about this area, on orders, for several days to keep an eye out for Japanese shipping, but more important at the moment, to be on hand to rescue downed aviators during the next few days of what was expected to be furious activity.

Her captain, Lieutenant Commander R. H. Bass, placed the submarine 20 miles southeast of Mili on the 19th. Just before dawn, when American carrier planes were supposed to be in the air in the area, a heavy fog rolled in, and then rain, which blew in from the east for two and a half hours.

Just before sunrise a plane came along about 1,000 yards astern while the submarine was on the surface. Bass dived, expecting an attack, but it must have been an American—there was no attack.

The submarine dived at 5:46, but was up at 5:55, down again at 6:33, when another unidentified plane came over, and back up at 6:40.

It was up again, down again, up again, down again, as the lookouts tried to identify friendly and enemy planes. At 10:53, on the surface, a pilot radioed down to them, via "Hello, Lifeguard. This is 41. No opposition over Mili."

That was a relief to Lieutenant Commander Bass. But by 11:00 he was seeing Bettys splashing in the water, and chasing them without success. At noon he had another air contact, and dived again.

And so it went all day long, as one wave after another of the planes from the carriers came in, bombed, strafed, and headed out for their carriers.

From time to time the *Plunger*'s crew witnessed bits of the attack, and saw and heard heavy explosions on the Japanese-held island. But mostly it was up and down, all day long, trying to maintain the lifeguard patrol for the American fliers without being destroyed by a Japanese bomber.

Bass surfaced just after twilight, and sent the *Plunger*'s radio message reporting activity for the day.

The submarine remained on the surface then during the night, patrolling west of Mili and watching the searchlights on the shore as they flashed up overhead, looking for the American planes that might be there, but were not.

On November 20, D-Day, four battleships, four cruisers, thirteen destroyers, and five carriers moved against Makin, escorting the half-dozen transports with the troops aboard.

At 5:00 in the morning, the atoll was visible from Kelly Turner's flagship, the *Pennsylvania*. Forty minutes later the ships and carriers were launching spotting planes and attack planes that swooped in over the beaches, dropping bombs and strafing.

But the Japanese were dug in on Makin. They had been hit by carrier raids for two days already and they had backed up off the beach, to points farther along where they would make their stands. Not that there were so many of them—but they were determined to fight.

On the day before, the Japanese had waited in their emplacements for the attack they knew must come from the moment they began to feel the might of the American air armada hitting them.

At 3:00 on the morning of this important November day, Chief Petty Officer Sasaki, platoon leader of the artillery unit assigned to Makin, sat in his dugout, awakened from sleep by enemy planes coming over. He counted thirty-two of them, and he fired his weapons at them, without hitting any.

After an hour or so, the planes withdrew.

But at 5:20 they were back again, twenty-seven of them this time. Again Sasaki and his men fired at the aircraft, but their weapons were hardly suited for the action. They were not successful in shooting one down.

At 9:00 in the morning another strike came, and then after noon another. By this time, the bombers had knocked out the island's basic communications system, and Chief Petty Officer Sasaki and his men could not communicate with headquarters until the attack was over and he could send a runner back.

At 2:45 in the morning, Petty Officer Sasaki saw the task force, shining in the moonlight offshore. He made out three battleships, two cruisers, three destroyers, and many other ships.

The enemy planes soon came over and began bombing, and the ships began shelling. "They were shelling all along the waterfront," he wrote in the diary he had been keeping since the action began the day before.

At 5:00 the bombing and shelling became so furious that Sasaki stopped trying to man his antiaircraft artillery and moved to safety.

"I assembled my men and we ran to the Eastern Observation Post for refuge. Then, gathering up the personnel of the post, we all ran for the air-raid shelter."

There they stayed, watching, as the enemy planes came over, some of them making reconnaissance, some bombing. He saw a group that he recognized as B-24 heavy bombers.

An hour later, Sasaki was even more shocked, stupefied, by the extent of the force used. "From both sides, inside and outside the lagoon, the enemy is pouring concentrated shelling and bombing into the area of our headquarters. . . . Bombs are dropping by the score. . . ."

At 7:00 in the morning the bombing and shelling stopped, but only for ten minutes. Then intermittent enemy bombardment began again.

The American troops were ashore by this time, and Petty Officer Sasaki and his men decided it was the hour for action.

"Now without stopping to rest, we determined that it is up to us to make a stand. I have twenty men under me. Suppose the Samurai does not kill himself when he is supposed to kill himself? It is dying, just for the joy of it that is disgraceful. . . ."

But then the shelling stopped suddenly, and Petty Officer Sasaki reconsidered. "We are not so badly off as we thought," he wrote.

Twenty minutes later he was again sunk in gloom. "The ships retire. We are almost completely wiped out. There is no ammunition left. . . ."

Another hour. "The enemy's heavy battleships retire to the east. We all shout Banzai for the Emperor's cigarettes, which are holding out very well."

And then came 8:45 that morning, with the army units easily ashore, and Sasaki and his men desperate in the face of the power opposed to them.

"We are all set to charge. Only Chief Petty Officers Shimizu, Shikayuma, and Sasaki and thirty able-bodied men are left. Practically all the fortified positions have been rendered useless. . . ."

The diary ended there on the morning of D-Day.

The landing boats had circled off the Makin beaches until the naval barrage let up, and then they moved in, the first touching shore at a few minutes after 6:30 that morning.

Since there was virtually no opposition (one machine-gun post on Beach Red manned by seven Japanese), Company L of the 165th Infantry had little trouble in moving forward. The real difficulty arose when a party of sixty Gilbert Islanders came down grinning and waving, to offer them coconuts and engage in conversation.

It hardly seemed like a war at all.

They did learn that there were supposedly 800 Japanese on the island, about half of them combat troops and the other half laborers.

And they moved forward, but slowly.

By midmorning they were going off from the western beach-head on the island (with no opposition). They were stopped completely by a combination of obstacles: a shell crater in the middle of the road, and fifteen Japanese soldiers manning a machine gun.

The progress was agonizing then. Eventually the fifteen Japanese were killed, but not before they had held up the advance for hours, and accounted for the death of Colonel Conroy, the commander of the assault landing force, who had been in front, urging his reluctant troops into action.

As evening came, the assault bogged down completely, and the soldiers, nervous in their first action, began firing indiscriminately—even at each other.

On Tarawa the story was still very different. The airmen had plastered the beaches and tree groves of Betio with everything they had, and the big ships had unleashed their heavy guns and blasted at all targets they could find. But the Japanese guns were extremely effective at this range, and the boats that milled about were hit, some of them seriously. Dead and wounded were in the boats offshore as well as lying in the water and on the beach.

Many of the men who had had to debark in water up to their necks were lucky. Some were not. Some made the beaches only to fall. But some got through, and they began to fight.

They crawled or ran or wriggled, and they found safe hiding

places on the pier, and soon enough behind stalled bulldozers and other equipment that had been meant to go right up and rout out the enemy soldiers.

Tanks stalled in the water, and the crews abandoned them. Then the Japanese began infiltrating back into the stalled equipment, hiding there, and waiting.

The marines kept on coming.

Petty Officer Oonuki drove his tank back to the admiral's headquarters blockhouse, stopped, and went inside. There he learned that his tank was one of two not knocked out by the aerial and gun bombardment of the last few hours.

He was to go back out, and use the tank for reconnaissance. The admiral's command post had been cut off from telephonic communication with the frontal defense units, and only by such observation and reports would he know what was going on.

Oonuki rounded up a scratch crew. Petty Officer Shiraishi came with him, and Seaman Ota volunteered.

So they got into the tank and headed down the main airstrip. The going was rough: bombs and shells had pitted the strip and the tank wobbled along through the debris and into the holes. Dust, debris, and heat had already affected the tank's mechanism, and now it threatened to quit entirely. Oonuki nursed it along, sputtering, as they headed down the strip.

They spotted a line of green-clad marines, racing across the taxi strip ahead of them. Ota was manning the 37mm gun, and he fired at them. Shiraishi trained the 7.7mm machine gun on them and fired a few bursts.

Halfway along the airstrip, the Type 97s engine finally quit. Petty Officer Oonuki did everything he had learned to do to get the machine going once more, but the engine would not catch.

Ota and Shiraishi kept firing, although the marines had taken cover on the other side of the airstrip, and there was nothing to shoot at.

Finally, the two gunners announced that they were about to run out of ammunition. Oonuki was ready to tell them it was time to bail out and leave the tank before they were either captured or cooked in it by the enemy's flamethrowers.

One more try—he got the starter going, and then the engine caught and the stalled tank came to life. He swung it around and began moving slowly toward the admiral's blockhouse.

The clutch was burned out, and the tank barely crawled. They felt like sitting ducks, exposed on a broad front, but they made it back to the blockhouse.

Inside they discovered the place was full of wounded.

They sat there in the candlelit room, for all the electric power was long since gone, dripping with sweat in the heat of jammed-up bodies, and waited.

Officers scurried to and fro, carrying papers that were apparently for burning outside. A captain stopped, called for attention, and held up a message blank.

They had just received a message from Tokyo, he said. It came from the Emperor himself.

"You have all fought gallantly. May you continue to fight to the death. Banzai!"

No one questioned it. The men inside the bunker felt a lift of pride, in what they had done for their Emperor and for Japan.

From time to time, officers and petty officers went rushing out of the shelter. Petty Officer Shiraishi, who had accompanied Oonuki on that last official mission, now came charging in waving a bloody Samurai sword.

He had just killed a dozen Americans, he bragged. He was going back into the fray. Who wanted to go with him? A few men got up and followed him out.

As the day wore on, the admiral and his staff decided their command post was useless. They must move to a place nearer the shore, so he could discover what was happening.

There seemed to be about 300 men in the shelter. An officer divided them into two groups, one to go with the admiral, and the other to go with the chief of staff. Petty Officer Oonuki was assigned to the chief of staff, and as tank driver he was to create a diversion so that the admiral could move to the new command post. The others would help.

Petty Officer Oonuki got back into his tank, with two new

companions, and they moved down the strip, firing the last of the ammunition left by Shiraishi and Ota.

The tank stalled, all three got out, and Petty Officer Oonuki stopped to wrench open the fuel valve. He had intended to drop a grenade in from outside, but as he got out a tremendous explosion blew the sand up all around him, and he forgot the tank, abandoned it, and ducked into a foxhole. It was full of dead men, so he went on, to another dugout. Here he found several men whom he knew, badly wounded, lying among several dead bodies.

At first, in exhaustion, they just lay in the shelter. Then, hungry and thirsty, they began to search for food and water.

Each man was supposed to have a canteen, but these had disappeared in the running and diving for cover that marked this first day of the battle.

They clawed into the sand until a bit of brackish water began to show, and then they clawed further, until they created a soupy puddle from which they could drink.

Time went by. Then the Japanese began to hear strange sounds outside, the crunch of grenades, the popping of guns, the whooshing explosion of flamethrowers.

Suddenly a clunking sound inside their shelter made them realize they were under attack. They stuffed a blanket into the observation slit, just in time, for it was ripped by an explosion. Grenades—the Americans were attacking them with grenades.

Then the Americans found an opening and trained a flamethrower on it. The interior of the shelter erupted in orange fire.

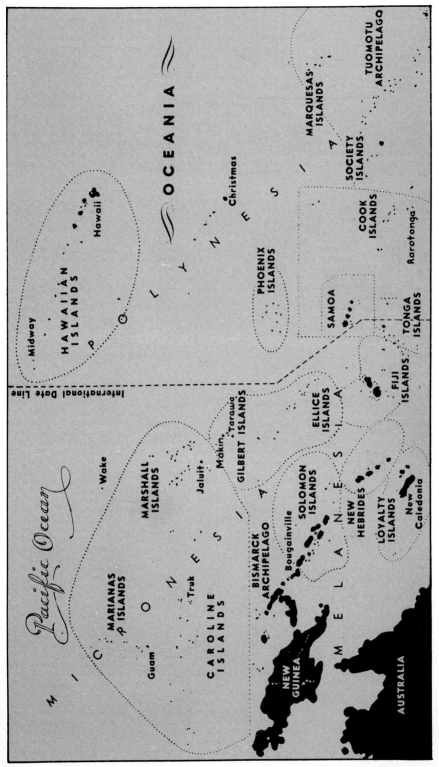

(New York Public Library Picture Collection)

At the beginning of 1943, the Americans were still beginners in the science of amphi
warfare; by the end of the war, the U.S. Pacific Fleet included battleships, carriers, cru
destroyers, transports and landing craft. Forces from all service branches were repres
(National Archives, Washington, D.C.)

The Japanese fleet, photographed on October 11, 1940, included battleships, aircraft ca
and cruisers, and was at that time superior in the Pacific. *(Wide World Photos)*

A Japanese-eye view of a U.S. Elco PT boat. *(New York Public Library Picture Collection)*

A Japanese cruiser, wrecked and burning after an attack by U.S. planes. *(New York Public Library Picture Collection)*

Left: Admiral Isoroku Yamamoto, head of the combined Japanese fleet, was the mastermind behind the attack on Pearl Harbor. Keenly aware that American naval forces had superior potential, he worked toward the construction of a stronger naval air-surface arm for Japan. He was killed in the Pacific in 1943. *(U. S. Navy)* Right: Betio Island in Tarawa was expected to be an easy conquest once naval gunfire had knocked out its shore defenses, but no one realized how much punishment the Japanese could take. *(The Bettmann Archive, Inc.)*

These Navy aerial gunners, standing beside a Dauntless dive bomber that operated from a carrier, participated in nearly all major Pacific engagements. *(Official U.S. Navy photograph, courtesy New York Public Library Picture Collection)*

Left: Admiral Chester W. Nimitz, Commander-in-Chief of the U.S. Pacific Fleet in charge of the new Central Pacific operation in 1943, set his sights on the Gilbert and Marshall Islands, the nerve center of Japan's defense system. Right: Vice-Admiral Raymond Spruance, Annapolis-bred and "regulation" through and through was chosen by Nimitz to be Commander of the new task force in the Pacific. *(National Archives, Washington, D.C.)*

Admiral Nimitz (second from left) at a conference with other high-ranking naval officers including Rear Admiral Forrest P. Sherman, USN (center), and Admiral William F. Halsey, USN (right), Commander of the Third Fleet. *(The Bettmann Archive, Inc.)*

The U.S. Coast Guards land from an LST. *(The Bettmann Archive, Inc.)*

Leaders of the Marine Corps assault on Tarawa hold a conference during the battle. Lieutenant David M. Shoup (center, holding map case) led the assault; seated at front is Lieutenant Colonel Evans Carlson; at left, standing with hands on hips, is Colonel Merritt A. Edson. *(The Bettmann Archive, Inc.)*

7
THE FIRST DAY

The landing vehicles had brought the marines into the lagoon and put them down in sight of the beach, some of them half a mile from the shore of the three landing beaches, Red One, Red Two, and Red Three.

What beaches?

For as the marines came in, swimming, paddling, walking on the bottom to get to the beach from their stranded vehicles offshore, the Japanese were shooting at them. And except for the wrecked vehicles and the pier, there was little cover. Captain Sugai's men had built a seawall 4 feet high, by driving Ensign Ota's coconut logs into the sand and then laying other logs across them. From the seawall down to the water, at this tide, there was a 20-foot strip of beach next to the pier. That was the beachhead of the Second Battalion of the Eighth Marine Regiment. It was typical of the situation on all the beachfronts.

Coming in, some of the marines went forward, over the sea-wall, to try to get at the machine guns placed to command the landing beaches. Behind the stalled vehicles, marines were al-ready stringing wire, setting up communications and command posts.

From their positions back on the island, the Japanese field

gunners were shooting well. They knocked out amtracs and LVTs, and kept their fire heavy on the incoming troops.

Then the sniping began.

All along the marines' perimeter, and sometimes behind it, the Japanese lurked in whatever cover they could. From deserted tanks, from concealed pillboxes, they sat and watched the marines go by, and then they began sniping.

The marines used TNT, grenades, and flamethrowers to rout them out, but with the bullets whizzing by and the crumping of the bigger guns overhead, it was not an easy task. The only way they could determine that a Japanese soldier was within shooting distance was to wait until somebody got shot.

Late in the morning aboard the *Maryland,* General Julian Smith and Colonel Edson were still standing there at the rail, eyes glued to their glasses, watching. Word came from flag plot, the admiral's communications center, that the beach had reported. The marines had established a beachhead.

General Smith rushed over to Colonel Edson and thrust out his hand.

"They've done it," he shouted.

Edson stood there quietly. He did not take his commander's hand.

"I'd rather wait, sir," he said.

Aboard the *Pennsylvania,* Kelly Turner's flagship, Holland Smith was worried. He had not expected anything easy at Tarawa, but now he sensed that it was not going very well.

An hour and a half after the landings, he had his first message from the beach. It came from General Julian Smith:

"Successful landings on Beaches Red Two and Three. Toehold on Red One.

"Am committing one LT [landing team] from division reserve. Still encountering strong resistance."

Holland Smith was uncomfortable, but not dismayed. Commitment of a section of the reserve so early was unusual.

The fact was that on Beach Red Three, where Major Henry

Pierson Crowe was in command, "toehold" just about sized up the strength of their command of the ground. The casualties kept coming in to the command post, to any point of concealment where they could be protected until they could be taken off the island and back to the ships. And in many ways Crowe was the best off of all the commanders ashore.

Behind those first waves of amphibian tractors, which got the assault troops in, the LCVPs and LCMs were piling up with the artillery and the tanks. For the estimates of the depth of water had been wrong—that was the big trouble now. In some places it was 3 feet. In some places it was 6 inches near the shore. The landing craft drew 4 feet.

These were the heaviest casualties, the people Robert Sherrod saw fall and die in the water as the Japanese snipers zeroed in on them. It was ironic that the assault waves, which had expected to catch it hardest, really had easier going than the reserve elements.

But Red Three was not alone. On Red Two, Lieutenant Colonel Amey's LCM stuck, and he first commandeered an amphibious tractor. When it was hung up by the barbed-wire entanglements the Japanese had erected in the area, he tried to wade in and was shot down by a machine-gun burst. His place was taken by Lieutenant Colonel Walter Jordan, who had come ashore as an observer.

Colonel Shoup and regimental headquarters also had a hard time coming ashore. Their landing craft ran into a hail of fire, and he struggled in along the pier, under continual fire, to set up the command post.

So it was very rough going. Aboard the *Maryland,* General Julian Smith knew it soon enough. Shortly after the end of the first hour, Smith committed another unit, the Third Battalion of the Eighth Marine Regiment, and sent it in to help Crowe. They started in, some 300 of them, and their boats grounded on the reef. The ramps came down and the men began wading in, sometimes in water that went over their heads. Some plunged into deep water and drowned. Others were killed by the renewed storm of Japanese fire and shells that sought them. Of the whole first wave of 300, perhaps 100 men got to the beach that day.

When they reached the beach they were scarcely better off. For there was no cover, and the Japanese fire was deadly. Nearly this whole third wave was wiped out—300 men gone.

In came the next wave, but it suffered the same fate, and when Colonel Shoup discovered what was happening he sent the order to stop landing men until further notice.

The beachhead, then, was in deadly danger within two hours of the beginning of the assault.

There was no time to worry about blame now—there would be endless investigations and discussions of the failure later—but the fact was that a whole team of British experts from the Gilberts, Australia, and New Zealand had indicated to the unknowing Americans that on this particular day at this particular hour there ought to be 4 to 5 feet of water over the reef.

And of course there was not, so men died.

General Julian Smith's problem was to sustain the momentum of the attack, lest the troops be pinned down on the beaches and lose heart. But how could he get the support forces in when they must cross 400 or 500 yards of water raked by Japanese machine guns and rifle fire before they could find the slightest bit of shelter?

During this vital period, neither General Smith nor Colonel Shoup could rely on visual observation from the ships offshore. The clouds of smoke and dust hung low over the island and prevented their telling what was happening. Colonel Shoup set up his command post in a spot protected from fire by a Japanese pillbox with live Japanese inside. But by noon, Colonel Shoup had made contact with the commanders of the various units ashore, except for Beach Red One. There the situation was still unknown.

On Red One, Major Michael P. Ryan organized the troops and created a fighting force from the remnants of several companies that had been almost wiped out. Here the hard training of the marines showed itself; these men adjusted to complete change of command and operating procedure under heavy fire without a whimper, and moved on to fight as though it had all been planned this way.

They consolidated the beachhead on Betio's "beak" (visualizing the island as a bird). They cleared a beachhead 500 yards deep and 150 yards wide. It was tiny but it gave them breathing room. They reached the antitank ditch the Japanese had dug 300 yards from the south coast of the island, and held that position until night forced them back to the beach.

One reason for their success was that Ryan had two tanks, which had reached the land without sinking in. Four others which were coming in at the same time had fallen into "potholes" and their engines had drowned out. For the purposes of the battle, they were lost.

Of the two that came lumbering ashore at Beach Red One, one soon was hit and began to burn. The other was also hit, but its forward machine gun continued to operate and it could maneuver. It was used all afternoon, and then put into position to protect the marines for the night as they settled down.

Aboard the *Maryland,* General Julian Smith added it all up late in the morning, and sent a message to Holland Smith on the *Pennsylvania* in Makin waters.

"The situation is in doubt," he said.

He wanted to commit the last of his reserves, the Sixth Regiment of the Second Marine Division, to the fight.

Aboard the *Pennsylvania,* Holland Smith and Kelly Turner conferred. General Smith was very much perturbed because it was too early, by any normal standards, to be committing the reserve. And yet he had enough faith in Julian Smith's judgment to realize that something was very much amiss or Julian Smith would not have made the request. "Situation in doubt"—dreadful, worrisome words.

Early in the afternoon, after Julian Smith had radioed Holland Smith at Makin, asking for permission to land the reserve regiment, because "the issue is in doubt"—that word was flashed to Admiral Spruance.

His staff was shaken. The last time the marines had used that term was just before the surrender at Wake Island in December 1941.

If the issue was in doubt, that meant the invasion was in grave danger.

Spruance's staff urged him to enter the operations: to send messages demanding decisions from Admiral Hill and General Smith.

Spruance refused. He had chosen these men, he said. They were in command. They knew their jobs. He would not interfere.

He watched as the horror unfolded. Finally it was apparent what had happened: the landing had run into an extremely low tide, as predicted (rather belatedly and lamely) by Major Holland, one of the British former officials from the Gilberts. In the days of planning the risk seemed negligible; now marines were falling and dying in the water, hundreds of yards from shore, and landing craft were hanging up on the reef, to become sitting ducks for the Japanese 5-inch and 8-inch guns.

LVTs began to burst into flames. Amtracs hit the beaches, and the machine guns opened up on them.

The horrible truth was in front of Spruance. The naval and aerial bombardments had done little, if anything, to the defenders. The Japanese were full of fight, and the whole invasion was in deep trouble.

It was apparent that disaster was almost on them. The careful communications plan went spinning, radio discipline collapsed, and captains and commanders began yelling over the airwaves all at once.

Aboard the *Maryland* the first 16-inch salvos from the big guns had jarred the radio equipment so that it was totally inoperative for some time. That meant Harry Hill and Julian Smith were completely out of touch with the marines ashore. For the moment, at least, they might as well be 1,000 miles away.

This was the worst hour for Admiral Spruance. He stood on

his bridge, watching through the binoculars, as the landing craft circled offshore in confusion, the coxswains who knew about the low water on the reef unsure what to do.

Between ship and land the smoke began to pile up, and it became even harder to see the beach.

Spruance stood. He waited.

And so the two commanders agreed that Julian Smith should have the last of the troops.

While this exchange was occurring, the fighting did not let up for a moment on the beaches. On Red Three, three Sherman tanks arrived, and then moved across to Red Two, where the troops were trying to reach the airfield, one of the major points of attack. Tanks were used to roll up to the pillboxes and fire pointblank through the openings. It was an effective technique, but had its dangers. The defenders could also lob grenades back into the tanks. And they did so. Before the afternoon was over, two of those tanks were knocked out.

All afternoon the marines' artillery lay just offshore, because of the difficulty of getting it in over the reef. Finally two gun sections were transferred to amphibian tractors, which could make the trip, and they came ashore with 75mm pack howitzers, just about dusk of this first day.

There were ironies and accidents aplenty on this day. The tanks suffered from friends as well as enemies. Four Shermans came ashore near the Burns-Philp pier, to lead the troops inland. One was knocked out by an American dive bomber. One was moving ahead, and suddenly dropped into an excavation. Another American plane zoomed low overhead, firing. Suddenly there was a tremendous explosion, and the tank and everything around it began to burn. The unlucky tank crew had fallen into a Japanese fuel dump and the American plane had set it afire around them.

A third of these four tanks was disabled by the Japanese anti-boat guns, 37mm guns that were equally effective against medium tanks.

The fourth, damaged by a shell, continued to fight the rest of the day.

The situation was, as Julian Smith said, in doubt.

It took Holland Smith and "Terrible Turner" only fifty minutes to approve the use of the remaining reserves. And so, with the Sixth Regiment of the Second Division as that last backup, Julian Smith sent his only other infantry troops into the line—the First Battalion of the Eighth Regiment.

He decided to commit them to the beach at the east end of the north shore. And the orders went out. But for some reason Colonel Hall, the regimental commander, did not receive the orders. So the last troops sat in landing craft, offshore, from midafternoon until midnight—waiting.

Late in the afternoon, Lieutenant Colonel Evans Carlson was sent from shore back to the *Maryland* by Colonel Shoup to give a picture of what was happening to General Julian Smith. What was happening was mostly confusion, which was saved from becoming disaster only by the magnificent performance of the individual soldiers. Because of mistakes, communications failures, and misunderstandings, the whole operation was completely out of kilter. The one thing that could be said positively was that the marines were ashore, hanging on, and that they knew how to fight and were not afraid to die.

One of those who had gone ashore at Beach Red Three by mistake in the confusion over the shallows was *Life* correspondent Robert Sherrod. He stayed around Major Crowe's command post for a time, watching the wounded come in, to be taken out to the ships as soon as they could be gotten away. Then he decided to head for Beach Red One, where he was supposed to have gone with his unit.

As he moved, he could see more than fifty disabled halftracks, tanks, and boats in the water. He moved behind the cover of the pier as far as he could, then ran 40 feet under Japanese fire, bullets whizzing about his head, to a big coral rock, and dropped behind it. And finally he found Second Battalion headquarters in a shellhole under the seawall.

And from here, Sherrod, who had been party to the higher discussions of strategy and tactics in days past, could see that the attack on Betio had certainly gone awry.

It was growing dark as he lay in the shellhole of the command post and listened to Colonel Jordan tell how it had been all day. The beachhead here was only 20 feet wide. Fifty yards to the west was Colonel Shoup's pillbox and headquarters (with the Japanese still inside), and there the beachhead might have been 75 feet wide.

And so they settled down for the night.

At Sherrod's command post the officers sent the men to dig their foxholes with the warning that the Japanese would probably come over to bomb during the night. And as the men moved to various points of safety and command of the area, to dig, Sherrod looked offshore in the failing light. He could see reinforcements coming in to the beach near the long pier, and he could hear the Japanese riflemen and gunners firing at them.

Sherrod and another correspondent dug their foxhole beside a coconut pillbox that contained four dead Japanese defenders.

Already, Sherrod noted in the comparative cool of evening, the bodies were beginning to stink.

In the foxhole, Sherrod estimated his chances of survival, and they did not seem very high. He estimated that the marines held "20 feet along perhaps one sixteenth of one half of one side of the island, plus a few men in shellholes on either side of the airstrip." The Japanese held all the rest of the island.

A gambling man would hardly take the marines at that moment.

The light carrier *Independence* had begun operating on D − 2 with Task Group 50.3, Rear Admiral Montgomery's force, and the pilots of the three squadrons involved had carried out their missions with an ease and skill that seemed routine at this stage of the war.

There was nothing unusual in the operation in those first three days; the task was to bomb and strafe land targets, and if some of the pilots felt that their bombs were not as effective as they should be, that matter would have to await the evaluation of higher authority.

Late on the afternoon of D-day, Captain R. L. Johnson was on the bridge, the ship was traveling almost due north at 20 knots, and it was time for the antisubmarine patrol planes to be picked up. At 4:25, a lookout sighted a submarine periscope a mile away. The captain ordered the *Independence* to flank speed, which was 25 knots, and signaled that he had seen a submarine.

Admiral Montgomery detached U.S.S. *Kidd* to hunt down the enemy.

Five minutes later, Captain Johnson changed his speed to 20 knots again, and changed course so that he could prepare to recover the planes. The carrier zigzagged for a time, but just before 6:00 that evening, the zigzagging was stopped, to let the planes land.

Two minutes later the telephone rang on the bridge. It was the combat information center, and the CIC had vital news. A large group of unidentified planes was approaching the formation of ships from the west—very low over the water.

By this time, American planes operating against the Japanese from carriers had a pretty good idea of basic Japanese torpedo-bombing tactics. One aspect was the low approach to avoid early radar detection, and another was the timing—late in the day, when the poor light could be expected to silhouette a ship to planes coming in from the west, but the setting sun would shine in the eyes of the ship's gunners while the Japanese pilots came in on them.

The report was from Lieutenant McMillan, flying plane C-7, a member of the antisubmarine patrol that was getting ready to land.

Scarcely had the captain put down the telephone when he saw them: fifteen Bettys coming in on the starboard beam, fast and low.

The button depressed, the racket flooded the bridge, and all the ship as general quarters sounded. Men began to run. Feet clattered on the ladders and the decks.

On the bridge glasses were focused on the western horizon,

where the planes moved in. They had already deployed into a line, and were heading for the formation. But their leader then made a judgment; they swept around and came in on the *Independence.*

In order to move in close to the formation and thus take advantage of combined antiaircraft fire, Captain Johnson turned the *Independence* left 20 degrees, which also presented the narrow stern instead of the broad beam to the approaching torpedo planes.

The Japanese saw, and as they came, three bombers split away from the formation and tried to move ahead to cut off *Independence's* motion. Captain Johnson ordered a swift change of course, to starboard, and then, as the planes moved around, back to port.

The maneuver was successful in bringing the diversionary planes into the range of U.S.S. *Hale,* whose gunners shot down one of them.

On the bridge, a lookout sighted a torpedo wake approaching from the starboard quarter.

The Japanese were coming in fast, just six minutes after they had appeared on the horizon. The gunners of the *Independence* opened up with everything they had. Those who manned the 20mm guns were cursing as the planes came in close; they could see that they were scoring hits, but the ordnance did not have the power to stop the enemy.

The racket was dreadful. On the bridge, the bursting of 5-inch shells from the guns of other ships, trying to knock down the bombers as they zeroed in on the carrier, made it impossible to transmit orders directly from bridge to pilot house, and several orders had to be repeated and relayed.

In the next minute—sixty seconds—six Bettys were shot down by the gunners of the *Independence,* three of them peeling off and falling into the sea less than 100 yards from the ship.

That first torpedo wake was followed by three others. Three passed astern of the ship, and crossed the wake, and the fourth passed close aboard the starboard side.

And then the fifth torpedo hit the *Independence* in the stern, on the starboard side.

Damage control went into action.

The damage-control people were already in helmets, flash-proof clothing, and gloves, and lying prone on the deck of the carrier.

All personnel of the carrier had been brought up at least to the second deck, except those whose action stations were below.

The *Independence* began to list immediately. She went to 12 degrees to starboard, and then righted herself to 7 degrees. The engineering department began to right the list, and the flight-deck crews moved the planes to help. The list was finally reduced to 3 degrees.

Fires had started here and there. Men with hoses and extinguishers rushed to help put them out. No. 7 40mm gun was completely blown up and overboard to port. One fighter, on deck, was bounced overboard by the explosion.

A few men were lost below, in the flooding of a number of compartments, but most made the upper decks when ordered. The explosion occurred about 30 feet from seven torpedoes stored in racks on the starboard side of the hangar—and they did not go up. Planes in the hangar had been spotted forward preparatory to recovering the last patrol, and so they were not in the way, to take the brunt of the explosion and perhaps cause more damage themselves.

Actually, the *Independence* was a very lucky ship; she had come through with less damage than one might have expected. Steering from bridge to rudder was lost in the explosion, so a change-over to aft steering was made. But she was steerable.

Very shortly, the *Independence* moved out, to travel under destroyer escort back to the safety of American waters. But so sturdy was she, and so well manned, that on the way back she was able to refuel a destroyer at sea when the smaller vessel went short of fuel.

Also, before entering port, two planes were launched from her flight deck, and the captain maintained that if there had been a little more wind he could have conducted ordinary flight operations all the way along.

Offshore, the rescue submarines were busy that day. The planes were striking the various islands to prevent the Japanese from moving air power over the beaches of Makin and Tarawa.

The submarine *Plunger* was operating off Mili, and according to instructions she surfaced when she saw many American planes above. That meant the air strike was on, and she should be alert to help if needed.

From 3:00 p.m. until nearly 4:15 she waited on the surface, and then she saw a plane smoking, flying along with two others. One of the undamaged planes returned to the submarine's position and indicated that the *Plunger* should head eastward. By voice radio the plane indicated that one pilot was down, 10 miles away.

The submarine began to move quickly, following the plane. A TBF was soon in contact, telling them to move to a position 10 miles from Knox Island.

It took the submarine more than two hours to reach the point indicated, and by then it was half an hour after sunset. The captain of the submarine put up two lookouts in addition to the usual four, and was on the surface all night long. The officer on the bridge used a police whistle, and the submarine moved dead slow, calling constantly for the downed pilots. Every half-minute the call went out, and the submarine crossed and criss-crossed the area. But it was a very dark night, and the lookouts saw nothing at all.

With the darkness on Tarawa came a new sort of activity. At sunset, the Japanese bombers from the Marshalls came in over the fleet to try to knock out some of the ships. The antiaircraft guns of the ships offshore began to fire, making red and yellow splashes and sharp lines shooting through the night. Then suddenly it all stopped, and the island and the night were quiet.

But not for long.

Within an hour the Japanese machine guns began firing, and the tracers stabbed across the beachheads where the marines had their heads down low. Also, oddly, from the shore came firing *into* the beachhead—and the marines realized that the Japanese from some of the pillboxes had swum out to the wrecked vehicles, and either brought their weapons or managed to use the weapons of the disabled American equipment, and were creating more damage, dealing more death in the night.

The Japanese staged a counterattack that night, and cut between Beaches Red Two and Red Three to take the long pier once again.

And then before dawn the Japanese sent over one of their big flying boats to observe the fighting on the island. The men who had fought at Guadalcanal remembered the sort of flying boat, which they called "Washing Machine Charlie" because of the somehow unplanely sound of the engines. Then the bomber circled back and forth across and around Betio, up and down the whole atoll, as if the men inside were making notes and sending back messages that would bring new attacks on the men in the foxholes.

Dawn came pinkly, and with it the Japanese machine guns again opened up, as if the gunners were somehow finding something new at which to shoot. The bomber circled, dropped some bombs, and then dropped some more, which fell into the water. Then it flew away.

The first day at Betio was over.

The second was about to begin.

8

THE SECOND DAY

As Julian Smith said later, if Admiral Keiji Shibasaki had brought his troops out in force that night to counterattack, they probably would have knocked the marines off their narrow beachhead, and the whole invasion might have failed.

But Admiral Shibasaki did not know how desperate was the situation of the men on Beaches Red One, Two, and Three. He had relied on telephonic communications, and if the barrage laid down by the gunners of the ships and the planes had done nothing else, it had torn up the telephone wires around most of the pillboxes and other installations. So Admiral Shibasaki, in his command post, was as much out of the picture as was Ensign Ito huddled in his concrete pillbox.

Meanwhile, as the night wore on, the commanders afloat and ashore were planning how best they might utilize their slender reserves to capture Betio with all possible speed, and as little loss of life as possible.

Colonel Elmer Hall and his reinforcements of the First Battalion, Eighth Marine Regiment, who had been forgotten out at the point of departure for shore all night long, were finally instructed to land on Beach Red Two and attack.

They made it in to a point about 500 yards from shore before the LCVPs grounded, and the men had to begin the long, deadly wading through the sea. En route, they were hit, as the men had been the day before, by fire from both sides. The casualties were heavy, but by 8:00 the men on their feet were ashore and ready to fight.

Their position was hampered considerably because they had lost their demolition charges and flamethrowers in the arduous passage over the reef. But it was made a bit better when they learned that the howitzers landed earlier had been brought together for a battery of five guns, and an earth embankment had been thrown up to protect the gunners.

The new troops had the benefit of these guns from the very beginning, because as they came wading in the howitzers zeroed in on the pillboxes that were firing on the beach and the water offshore and knocked out several of the machine guns.

On this second day, marines were going to try to fight across the island, and then down toward the men on Red One beachhead.

The morning was spent in such preparation.

Meanwhile on Makin, considering the difference in number of defenders, the army troops were making almost abysmal progress.

After the first of the 6,400 army troops landed early on the morning of D-Day, they made so little progress it seemed remarkable. Considering the opposition, Holland Smith would have expected the island of Butaritari to have been secured by dusk on D-Day. But not only was this not the case—the troops seemed totally disorganized.

Holland Smith was particularly annoyed to learn that by the end of the day, the soldiers still had made no effort to recover and return to the ships the body of their commanding officer, Colonel Conroy. Nor was the body returned on this second day, as the fighting began again.

Worried as Holland Smith was about the progress of events on Tarawa, he was still bound to the Makin operation. "Terrible

Turner" was in charge, and Turner refused to let Smith go on over to the trouble spot. Not until Makin was secure, he said; then Smith could go anywhere he liked.

So on the second day, Holland Smith went ashore with his aides, Major Woodrum and Captain Asbill, to make his own estimates of the situation as it developed.

The beach was quiet—there was not a Japanese in sight. As he drove along, watching the troops in the open unloading supplies, a company of riflemen came through, firing to the right and left of the road, forcing the unloading parties to take cover.

Holland Smith jumped down from his jeep and found the lieutenant in command.

What was he firing at? asked the general.

He was trying to clear out snipers, said the lieutenant.

Smith lost his temper. He pointed out in no uncertain terms that there were no Japanese in the area, and that the rifle company had best get up front, several thousand yards away, where something was happening.

The lieutenant insisted that he keep on.

And then "Howling Mad" Smith, who had been intelligent enough to come ashore without any rank insignia so he would not become a sniper target, revealed his identity.

"If I hear one more shot from your men in this area," he said, "I'll take your damn weapons and all your ammunition away from you."

The area quieted down.

As for the fighting, that day it consisted largely of consolidating the beachheads. But the Japanese were stout resisters here as at Tarawa, even though their numbers were far fewer. Tank-infantry teams had to work with flamethrowers and demolitions to clean out the pillboxes and prepared positions.

Smith made his tour, and went back to the command post to report to Turner.

"Enemy losses very heavy, own light. Consider situation in hand."

Still, Turner insisted that General Smith stay to wait for the end of the Makin action, and in his concern, the general's irritation with the army for moving so slowly began to build. He was incensed about the failure of the soldiers to recover Colonel Conroy's body, particularly when there was no danger in doing so. He sent a "rocket" of a message to Ralph Smith, commander of the division, ordering him to do so—and in itself that was very much of a reprimand.

He was eager to get to Tarawa, where the trouble was.

And it was true that there was plenty of trouble on Tarawa on D+1.

Colonel Shoup's plan for the second day called for the new troops landing to move westward toward the Red One beachhead, and what was left of the First and Second Battalions of the Second Marines to drive across the island, while Major Crowe's unit was to reduce an enemy pocket that had been discovered at the base of the Burns-Philp pier.

The Third Battalion of the Second Marine Division was to go to the far end of the island, called Green Beach, and be sure the Japanese were driven from that point.

Major Hays had one medium tank, but he had no flamethrowers; they had been dropped in the water. He tried to move ahead, but without the flamethrowers the Japanese pillboxes seemed impregnable. So his advance was slow and tortuous, not at all satisfactory to the major or anyone else.

Major Kyle's First Battalion was to move across the airstrip to the ocean shore, from the lagoon where they had come in.

They had to make use of whatever weapons they could find, and they were lucky. They had secured several old-fashioned water-cooled .30-caliber machine guns, and these were useful for keeping the Japanese heads down. They also found some .50-caliber machine guns on the beach, and fought with these. They were lucky to have them, because the Japanese moved machine guns into position to prevent the other marines on the shore from reaching Kyle's men and reinforcing them with weapons or supplies.

The Japanese, hampered seriously by lack of communications and the heavy bombardment of the first day, were still well organized and defending themselves energetically. As the fresh troops came in to the beach, the Japanese opened up on them with field guns. They would knock out a landing craft, and then when the marines started swimming in the water, the machine guns would open up on them. The Japanese also had some mortars in action.

They had sought every sort of concealment, from the broken-down tanks to an outhouse perched out over the water. The marines found that outhouse in the morning, and smashed it with mortar fire. The machine gun that was lacing the water suddenly stopped as the timber blew through the air.

All this while, from morning on, the destroyers stood close by and fired on the Japanese positions beyond the marines' perimeter. The carrier-based fighters came in to strike the enemy, and they made particular attempts to strafe and smash a rusted-out hulk of a freighter. The Japanese had swum out during the night and located a machine gun in the rusted hulk, and it was dealing death to the men in the water as they tried to come in over the reef.

One Hellcat after another swooped down low, its guns spitting, and then came back up. But the machine guns still fired.

Then came Hellcats carrying small bombs, and they tried to zero in on the enemy position. Two of the bombers missed, but one did not. The hulk erupted in a sheet of flame, but only one of a dozen fighters that came in carrying bombs managed to hit the target. The others all missed, one by 200 yards.

The trouble this day came from the snipers who had managed to conceal themselves behind the marines' lines. They gave the marines hell all day long, and they were as hard to find as beetles in a grasspile.

As the marines managed to edge inland, the coconut trees became the big problem. On the first day they had spent a good amount of attention on the coconut trees, knocking snipers out by the process of trial and error. But on the second day, they found the trees that had been cleared the day before were again infested, and the job had to be done over again, while marines were shot, wounded, and killed.

The positions were still insecure.

Colonel Shoup, the commander, still had his command post 15 yards inland from the beach. It was a hole in the sand behind that Japanese pillbox. The pillbox was 40 feet long, 8 feet wide, and 10 feet high, made of coconut logs at least 6 inches in diameter, piled in two tiers, 3 feet apart, with the inner space filled with sand. And the whole top was covered with sand. It was a marvelous protection against shelling, and had done very well, for when bombs hit beside such pillboxes they simply threw more sand up on them. It took a direct hit from a heavy bomb to knock one out.

If the Japanese had failed to take advantage of opportunity and attack on the night before, they were not repeating the error this day.

The First Battalion of the Second Marines started an advance toward the south coast and reached the area, taking an abandoned strongpoint some 200 yards long. But they had hardly jumped down into the Japanese trenches than they were subjected to an attack by the Japanese, and barely beat it off.

Lieutenant Colonel Jordan now came to this point with his seventy-five men, the remaining men of the Second Battalion who had managed to get ashore in the original position on Red One. They joined Kyle's 135 men, and now hoped to move along to link up with Crowe near the Burns-Philp pier.

But the going was desperately slow. The amphibious tractors came inshore now, picked up wounded marines, then took them back to the shore and out to the ships for safety.

The marines pressed on. Kyle managed to cross the airstrip and take command of a perimeter along the south coast of the island, although strong Japanese positions lay within 25 yards of the marines on east and west. The Marines were in control, but barely.

Major Crowe's unit found the fighting very hard and made

little headway on D + 1. To the east of the Burns-Philp pier there were just too many fortified Japanese positions, which could only be cleaned out with tanks, flamethrowers, and demolition charges, all of them in short supply. They advanced to the main airfield runway, but had to fall back as night began to lower, lest they be cut off from the rest of the battalion. So they went back to the Burns-Philp pier, and there they fought off a succession of Japanese infiltration attempts during the night, and strengthened the position of the morning.

Thus the Makin beachhead, as night fell, extended from 400 to 500 yards along the coast of the lagoon, on both sides of the long pier. The Americans had not yet taken the airfield, so there was a gap of 250 yards separating the south perimeter from that of the west. The Red Two and Red Three beachhead had been enlarged, but there were still gaps in it, and still plenty of opportunity for the Japanese to infiltrate—which they began to do with sundown.

On the west, Green Beach, the western side of the island, was taken by Ryan and his men, in the face of several boat guns, machine guns, and two 5-inch naval guns. Ryan's success was the brightest spot in Julian Smith's day, for with the capture of the west end of the island, for the first time in the invasion, reinforcing troops could be landed without coming under withering Japanese fire.

And the plan was to land the Sixth Marines, the last of the reserves, just as soon as it became apparent where their weight would be felt most strongly.

This was a matter that caused some spitting and cursing ashore.

"That damned Sixth is cocky enough already," one officer told Correspondent Sherrod as they crouched in Colonel Shoup's command post. "Now they'll come in and claim they won the battle."

It was not so long before that other marine units had evened the score—at least partly—with the arrogant Sixth by telling the New Zealand girls that the fourragère the Sixth's men wore on their shoulders was a badge of venereal disease. But it would be

a time yet, before the Sixth arrived, and there was plenty of glory
—and death—for all.

Correspondent Sherrod sometimes had the feeling that he and
those around him were the only ones left alive in the whole
invasion force. That feeling was reinforced during the day when
a Japanese soldier reached out from an air vent in the pillbox
behind the command post and shot a marine in the leg. Finally
everyone realized they were sitting on top of a nest of Japanese,
just 3 feet of coconut and concrete and sand separating them
from God knew how many of the enemy.

But late in the day, Sherrod encountered reinforcements of his
own kind: he and Bill Hipple of the Associated Press moved back
down to Major Crowe's beleaguered position, and there they
met up with Associated Press photographer Frank Filan and
United Press correspondent Richard W. Johnston, a figure so tall
in his fatigues that he would have made a fine target except that
his figure was as skinny as his mustache.

They amused themselves and comforted one another by telling stories on themselves and other correspondents. Don Senick,
the newsreelman, Johnston claimed, should get the Purple
Heart, because he had been sitting under a coconut tree when
a bullet hit the trunk above his head and dropped hot on his leg.

This sort of joke did something to take away the horror all
around them, the dreadful calm disinterest of death in combat,
where one marine was not so lucky: he was standing behind a
coconut tree when an American 75mm howitzer shell exploded
on the trunk, and fragments killed him.

By evening, there were certain encouraging signs that raised the
spirits of marines and correspondents alike. The first jeeps came
onto the island, towing 37mm antitank guns that could be invaluable in knocking out the pillboxes. And at regimental headquarters, Colonel Shoup at last could say, "Well, I think we are
winning," even though everyone knew the Japanese were still
fighting and would continue to fight.

During the afternoon, General Julian Smith had two reports

that Japanese had been seen wading across the shallow lagoon to the island of Bairiki, so he diverted the Second Battalion of the Sixth Marines to that island, to be sure that the Japanese did not get solidly dug in.

In fact, there were fifteen Japanese on that island, with a machine gun. When the marines came under fire, Smith called for an air strike, and a plane came in and began to strafe the position where the Japanese were reported.

That afternoon the marines on Betio were complaining about the incompetence of the air people. "They haven't hit fifty people in two days," one grimy fighter grumbled.

But here on Bairiki, the single Hellcat created a spectacle as impressive as a Roman circus. One lucky shot hit a can of gasoline in the Japanese pillbox; it went up with a flare and a whooshing explosion, and all fifteen Japanese soldiers were roasted in a structure that had suddenly turned into an oven.

The Second Battalion of the Sixth Marines landed without any opposition at all. It was so quiet some of them felt foolish when they did not find a single live Japanese defender on the island.

Even with the advantage of being able to land on a cleared beach, the First Battalion of the Sixth Marines had its problems. It was bringing in tanks: when the men went to bring them out, they discovered them buried under masses of supplies in the bottoms of the transports.

When the marines got into their rubber boats, they found they were 1,200 yards off the beach and had to be towed in all the way by landing craft.

When they reached the beach, they found it was mined. An LVT carrying water, food, and medical supplies was the first to hit a mine, and was destroyed. The rest of the First Battalion moved to the northern portion of the beach.

The battalion was ashore by dark and was planning a night attack when an order came from division headquarters to hold up until the morning. That would give the men time to sort the tanks from the piles of supplies, and to make it in to shore to support the attack.

So as evening came, Colonel Shoup could say guardedly to General Julian Smith: "Casualties many. Percentage dead not known. Combat efficiency—we are winning."

Back aboard Turner's flagship, the word was passed to "Howling Mad" Smith, who was ashore on Butaritari, fuming at the incompetence of the army. At least he knew his marines were doing all right.

9

THRUSTS AND
COUNTERTHRUSTS AT SEA

The Gilberts invasion caught the Japanese by surprise, because they had really been expecting action in the more important Marshalls. But even in this they would have been sorely hampered by losses in their air power. They had been counting on carrier and land-based planes to turn the tide, but the carrier raids on the islands and the losses at Rabaul in early November made it impossible for the Japanese airmen to react.

Admiral Koga, the commander of the Combined Fleet, knew the fleet was already reeling from the blows struck at Rabaul and Bougainville. One reason for the immense destruction of aircraft by the American bombers at Rabaul was that Koga had just a few days before moved all his carrier-based planes ashore for a major strike against American ships in the New Guinea area.

The battle of Empress Augusta Bay, early in November, had deprived Japan of half a dozen of her warships, sunk or damaged. And then the air strikes at Simpson Harbor put four more cruisers out of action and tied up two others escorting them back to Truk.

Even though in early November Tokyo knew from the heavy

air attacks on Tarawa that the Gilberts would be the next landing target, there was virtually nothing they could do except cheer Admiral Keiji Shibasaki on in his defense efforts at Betio. They never told the admiral that his hopes for air support were now forlorn, that the heavy guns of Admiral Kurita's cruisers could not be brought up to help him.

On November 19, while the carrier planes were still softening up Betio and the invasion forces had not yet appeared, Admiral Takagi aboard his flagship at Truk was pressed for help. Takagi was the submarine force commander, and he represented just about all the warships that Japan could throw into this battle.

Takagi began to act.

First he ordered *I-169* to Makin from its patrol area between Hawaii and the Marshalls. The submarine captain, Lieutenant Commander Zenshin Toyama, indicated that the boat was near the end of its endurance, but that made no difference. The need was too great. Takagi laid out an interception line that ran north of Makin and sent *I-169, I-19, I-40,* and the smaller submarine *RO 38* to the area.

I-19, which was equipped with an airplane, had just returned from a reconnaissance mission; the plane had flown over Pearl Harbor and checked the shipping situation. It was hurriedly put into service again and sent to sea. *I-40* was a brand-new submarine, just down from Tokyo and scarcely through with its shakedown cruise.

RO-38 was also a new submarine. Its captain, Lieutenant Commander Shunki Nomura, was serving on his first cruise as a submarine commander.

Takagi sent many confusing orders. First he established one line of deployment, and then another. And Lieutenant Commander Yamamoto in *I-35* was a part of that picture.

On November 21, he was coming very close to Tarawa, and he surfaced that night and sighted a large enemy task force.

When the invasion began on D-Day, the naval vessels off Tarawa's shore had been put on the alert to expect aerial counterattack from the Japanese. They were alert, so much so that when a single plane came in toward the fleet at 300 feet that afternoon, the gunners opened fire and put a ring of steel around it.

Luckily their shooting was not very good, because the plane was actually one of the *Maryland*'s observation planes, bringing Lieutenant Colonel Jesse Cook of the Second Marine Division to the fleet. The plane landed to escape the fire and stayed down on the water all night long, before the pilot felt it was safe to taxi to the battleship and deposit his passenger.

It was the second day before the Japanese were able to offer any kind of support at all to the defenders of Betio.

Early in the morning, just before dawn, eight Japanese planes showed up, but their pilots had been badly briefed. They came in over Betio, dropped their bombs without any apparent mission in mind, and soared off to their bases in the Marshalls.

That was the extent of the Japanese support of Admiral Shibasaki that day.

Admiral Hill and his captains were on the alert for an air attack from Mili or Maloelap, but it did not materialize that day. Mili and Jaluit were the two Marshall atolls nearest the Gilberts, but they were in no position to respond to the American attacks. For two days the American carriers had sent their planes over these islands and plastered them with bombs and laced their sands with machine-gun fire.

On November 21, D + 1, Admiral Hill learned that one of the escorting destroyers reported a submarine contact, and he left two of his destroyers behind to deal with it. They spent the whole day chasing echoes and firing depth charges, and at the end of it came back to announce that they thought they had damaged the submarine. But the Japanese records did not indicate any such activity at that time.

The carrier force also found a big Mavis four-engined flying boat and shot it down.

D + 1 ended with the Japanese totally unable to help their beleaguered comrades in the Gilberts.

All night long on November 20, the submarine *Plunger* continued to search for the downed aviator it had been sent to rescue, but without success.

Just before 6:00 in the morning the captain took the *Plunger* down. It was quite usual to dive at dawn; the enemy might find them in the early light and it was very difficult to see into the air. Also, it was always wise to begin the day with the boat in trim, and the way to check it was to dive.

Back on the surface in less than an hour, the *Plunger* headed out in search once more. She headed for Knox Island to establish her position, and steamed in an expanding square, the tracks of the succeeding legs being a mile outside those of the previous ones.

And as they moved, they listened to the radio, which told them of new strikes on Mili.

By 11:00 in the morning, the *Plunger*'s captain had decided the search for the downed aviator was futile. Perhaps he had been rescued, but more likely he had simply vanished in the maw of the ocean.

So the captain shaped a course for Maloelap, which would take them south and west of Mili, so he could keep an eye out for any downed aviators. Since the ship was in enemy waters, he had three surface lookouts and two men with their glasses focused on the sky.

At 1:00, the submarine had a message.

"Hello, Lifeguard . . . I have a message for you. . . ."

But the radio communications were not working satisfactorily, and the *Plunger* could not reply on a frequency the other could pick up.

Two torpedo bombers began to circle the submarine, and Captain Bass sensed that they were trying to show him another pilot was down somewhere. But where?

They ran into a squall, and through the blinding rain began to signal by searchlight to the planes.

"Where is the plane down?"

But the planes could not answer their searchlight communications.

One of the planes came over and made a message drop, and then another, but the water was too choppy, and the submarine could not locate the plane, if there was one; the men could not get in touch with the planes above. It was a very frustrating day. That evening, the *Plunger* sent a message back to Pearl Harbor, telling Admiral Lockwood that they could hear on frequency 6835, but could not answer. That message was sent to the carriers from Pearl Harbor that night.

Next morning, D+2, the *Plunger* was still searching for that downed aviator of two days earlier, without result. Shortly after dawn the men on the deck of the submarine saw fires on Mili, and watched the raid in progress.

At 8:00 in the morning the *Plunger* had a message that a survivor had been spotted about 23 miles from Knox Island, and the submarine headed out. On the way planes helped direct her, correcting her course, and two hours later, the submarine neared the pilot.

During the submarine's approach, a pair of planes circled the downed pilot and then came to beckon the submarine, but then the planes ran low on gas and had to head back to their carriers.

The *Plunger* moved in cautiously, for there were a large number of blips on the radar; there was no way to know if they were friend or foe.

Captain Bass waited for more American planes to appear to guard the downed pilot until they could pick him up, but none came. He had radar contacts at as little as 5 miles away. Who were they, these other pilots—American or Japanese?

Until Bass knew, it would be foolhardy to attempt the rescue. The captain would not put any men on deck until he knew what was going on—he might have to dive on short notice, and any men left on deck were almost certain to be lost.

Just before 11:30 the men on the submarines sighted the downed pilot in his rubber boat on the crest of a wave, about a mile away from them. They turned, and soon had him close off the port bow. And just as they headed up, a Zero came in at them out of a rain squall in a shallow dive. Simultaneously Captain Bass sounded the diving alarm and gave the order to clear the bridge.

The lookouts and the captain leaped for the hatch as the Zero came in strafing. The Japanese pilot was good; his bullets laced the length of the submarine, toward the bridge, as the captain dropped down the hatch, last man in, and the bullets clanged off the bridge as the hatch cover was pulled down.

From his little rubber boat, the downed pilot saw the Zero turn over in a quick pullup and roll over and reverse field, then come in strafing again, snap around once more, and make a third pass at the submarine just as the periscope shears went under water.

Down they went, to 140 feet, and leveled off.

The captain then had time to breathe. He checked. The executive officer, Lieutenant William George Brown, had been wounded by the strafing. Pharmacist's Mate Arthur Mullinix began to give him first aid. And then the captain learned that five others were wounded.

It was nearly half an hour before the *Plunger* returned to the surface to make another attempt to rescue the downed pilot. The Zero pilot either had not seen him or had shown compassion, for the man in the raft was still there, drifting, waiting.

Gingerly the submarine came to periscope depth and sighted the pilot, and when no planes were detected, it came up to the surface. In a few moments, two of the ship's officers helped Lieutenant (J.G.) Franklin George Schwarz out of his rubber boat and onto the firm footing of the submarine deck.

At full speed the *Plunger* headed south, searching for medical attention for the wounded men. The captain did not yet know how badly they were injured. It would be thirty hours before the wounded were taken from the submarine, but the injuries were superficial; all the men would recover nicely.

Meanwhile, the Japanese submarine *I-35* was moving in the waters off Tarawa. She had arrived on the evening of the 22nd, and had tried to enter the lagoon, but she was spotted by a destroyer and a plane, which came in to depth-charge her.

The destroyer dropped two depth charges and came very

close. Lieutenant Commander Yamamoto had dived deep, but the depth charges knocked out the lights and broke crockery in the galley.

Yamamoto stayed down for two and a half hours in the darkening night. He moved east and then back north to the lagoon, but could not enter. He moved north, and then south again. Still he did not dare to enter.

That night they saw a transport ship entering the lagoon, obviously taking supplies to the American marines ashore. Yamamoto tracked it, but he could not get into position to fire any torpedoes.

So the night passed.

Just after 5:00 in the morning, Yamamoto brought *I-35* to the surface. He saw no enemy ships or planes. Suddenly out of the clouds came two American planes zooming down. Yamamoto gave the order to clear the bridge and to dive, and as they went down the bombs dropped in their wake.

Yamamoto moved away from the danger zone, outside the destroyer screen that shielded the attacking forces.

At 11:00 that morning, *I-35* was east of the destroyer screen, at a depth of 65 feet, when suddenly the sound of speeding propellers shocked Yamamoto to attention.

Aboard the destroyer *Gansevoort,* the sound man reported to the bridge that he had a contact, and the destroyer wheeled and began to bear down on it at high speed.

Gansevoort came in and began dropping depth charges in the location of the contact. *I-35* went down to 260 feet, but as she went the depth charges were falling around her.

The lights went out. Then bulbs began shattering in the sockets from the concussion. The submarine began to shake. She sprang leaks in the plating.

The destroyers *Meade* and *Frazier* now came up to help. They roamed back and forth above the hapless submarine, stopped and silent in the depths. Each time they passed the point where she lay they dropped depth charges—altogether nearly seventy of them.

Yamamoto took her deeper, to 390 feet, but he could not escape. The instruments in the conning tower shattered from the concussion, and the gauges broke in the control room. The clocks broke down.

At this depth the packing around the diving planes came loose, from the changing pressure, and the rivets began to give, weakened by the constant pounding. The hull ruptured, and then the fuel tanks broke. The submarine began to take on water with alarming speed.

Yamamoto tried to move, but now discovered that the depth charging had cost him control—the rudder was not operating.

One final attack caused the submarine to nose down at an angle of 20 degrees, and Yamamoto knew he could not take her deeper; the pressure would crush the hull. So he blew the tanks and came to the surface, hoping to start the diesel engines and run away from the enemy ships.

It was a forlorn hope. As he surfaced he saw all around him the destroyers and cruisers of the enemy, and as the conning tower broke water the surface ships began to hurl a devastating fire at the submarine.

Two of the cruisers launched their float planes with bombs, and they came over, bombing and strafing.

A destroyer's shell wrecked the conning tower. A bomb exploded the ammunition locker of the deck gun.

As the submarine broke water, the gun crew began piling up the ladder of the conning tower to get on deck and man their guns. But the trainer, the pointer, and the gunnery officer were all killed in the attempt.

Other men went out, and they too fell beneath the hail of lead and flame.

Superior Petty Officer Ichiro Yamashita pulled himself out of the wrecked conning tower and made it onto the deck; he headed for the deck gun. But he never reached it—he was felled by a bullet from one of the strafing planes, and dropped unconscious.

First Class Petty Officer Shigeto Ohata was just behind Yamashita. His duty was at the diving-plane control when the ship was submerged, but on the surface he helped man the machine gun. He headed for his post, but he too was knocked down by a bullet or shrapnel, and fell unconscious.

Second Class Petty Officer Takashi Kawano was assigned to the deck gun, and he too headed for his post. But he saw that the ammunition locker had exploded, and he decided he would man the .50-caliber antiaircraft machine gun. He headed for it, reached the gun, and armed it. Just then one of the planes came in strafing, and Kawano felt a shock and then saw blood on his right hand. Two fingers had disappeared, shot off.

Then another bullet struck him, and he fell to the deck and could remember nothing more.

The planes strafed and bombed, and the guns of the ships found the submarine with accuracy. Men poured onto the deck and died. The captain came up, and was shot down. The submarine took in water. The *Frazier* charged in and rammed *I-35*, and in a few moments she sank, leaving three men in the water. Kawano came to and found himself clinging to a piece of wreckage.

The destroyers came up then and rescued the three survivors —the only ones left alive of a crew of eighty-one men and nine officers.

Captain James Jones was assigned to lead a small reconnaissance force to Abemama atoll. They had sailed on the submarine *Nautilus,* scheduled to land on the night of November 19 to determine whether or not the atoll was heavily defended. No one thought so. Aerial photographs had indicated there were virtually no defenses at all.

The marines boarded the submarine at Pearl Harbor, but then the *Nautilus* had a job to do at Tarawa—she was to watch for Japanese shipping—and so they went to that point. After the *Nautilus* left Tarawa and surfaced to make the run of 76 miles to the little atoll more quickly, she was spotted by the destroyer *Ringgold,* and the *Ringgold* attacked her, as has already been recounted.

The *Nautilus* arrived off Abemama before dawn on November 20. Jones and his men embarked in rubber boats and landed on one of the five islands of the outer curve of Abemama—the five together strung out rather like a half bracelet. They intended to land at the base of the bracelet on the island called John, but the current moved them down to the absolute end of the bracelet, to the island called Joe. There they found nothing. They crossed over the narrow waterway to John, and ran into a three-man Japanese patrol, ambushed it, killed one Japanese, and moved to the next little island, Orson. Three islanders met them and informed them that there were about twenty-five Japanese in defensive positions on the southern tip of the next island, Otto.

By this time it was November 23, and Jones felt that he should take the position. He moved against it, but the Japanese had organized their defense well; fire from their rifles and Nambu machine guns drove the Americans back. Jones then decided to use strategy.

Next morning the *Nautilus* moved in and shelled the Japanese on Otto with her deck gun, thus attempting to attract and hold their attention. The plan then was for Jones and his men to disengage, get into the rubber boats, bypass the stronghold, and attack from the rear.

But the Japanese were shrewd and brave. They kept firing steadily on the boats every time anyone went near them and pinned the Americans down.

Late that day a destroyer came up and began firing into the Japanese position. That is how the day ended, in stalemate, with the Americans using two warships and a superior force of men to fight two dozen Japanese.

That night it was quiet. Next morning, early, an islander came across, and reported to Jones that all the Japanese were dead!

How could that be?

Jones and his men went patrolling and soon discovered the fact. Four of the Japanese had been killed in the bombardment. The remaining eighteen had committed suicide in the night, sure the Americans would land men in force from the destroyer on the next day.

The marines had lost two men killed and one wounded. Abemama was taken.

On the night of November 21, General Ralph Smith asked for permission to land troops on Kuma Island, north of Butaritari in the Makin atoll, to cut off the Japanese retreat.

He had asked this before—in fact he had wanted to put troops ashore there on D-Day—but since such a landing was not a part of the original plan, Holland Smith had refused the change.

He and Admiral Turner had conferred and agreed that no subsidiary landings were in order until it was certain that the Japanese could be driven from Butaritari, and that island made secure.

On the third day it was so certain that the fighting was nearly over on Butaritari that there was no further objection. So a detachment of the 105th Infantry went ashore on Kuma in LVTs, ready to fight—and found nothing there but another welcoming party of Gilbert Islanders, who grinned and waved and offered them coconuts.

But still, the army infantry made slow going on Butaritari, much to the disgust of Holland Smith, who was hourly fretting to be on his way to Tarawa, where the trouble was.

On November 23, the Third Battalion of the 165th Infantry came out of reserve and crossed the eastern tank trap, which the Japanese had crossed two nights earlier. Beyond the tank trap the island was heavy with vegetation, which meant good vantage points for snipers.

At night, the Japanese infiltrated the American positions and attacked in small groups. But each attack was beaten off. The soldiers were learning. In the morning they found fifty-one dead Japanese in front of the positions of the battalion. They had lost three killed and twenty-five wounded during the night.

So on the morning of November 23 the soldiers swept to the end of the island, without meeting any further resistance.

General Ralph Smith's men then began counting the casualties. The Army had 218, sixty-six of them killed or dead of wounds. About 450 Japanese had been killed; one Japanese soldier was captured and 104 Korean laborers surrendered.

At 11:00 General Ralph Smith signaled Admiral Turner off-shore: "Makin taken. Recommend command pass to commander garrison force."

Long as it had been, and incompetent as he believed the army to be in its operation here, General Holland Smith was relieved and pleased at the message. Now he could leave the task force and get over to Tarawa where he belonged.

10
THE THIRD DAY

On the evening of the second day, Major Crowe had looked sourly about the beachhead. He cursed the planes bombing and strafing and commented that they had not done anything worthwhile in two days.

The biggest obstacle he had, which kept him pinned to the beach, was a big blockhouse, covered on one side by a steel shelter and on the other by a concrete pillbox. The blockhouse was formidable. It should have been—it was Admiral Shibasaki's command post, and he was there.

He had tried to get to the smaller post at the shore, but he had failed, and so he was spending the battle in his old place, the most formidable spot on the island.

All afternoon of the second day the marines had launched attacks against the blockhouse, without success. The Japanese in the area seemed to be coming at them constantly—the marines could not figure out how. But there they were, stopping Lieutenant Alexander Bonnyman and his engineers from getting close enough to hurl satchel charges into the openings, or to use flamethrowers effectively.

In the evening, frustrated, Crowe had called for a naval strike against the blockhouse, and a destroyer had come in so close some of the marines thought she would run aground. The destroyer began to fire, and laid in some eighty 5-inch shells. Crowe watched, still sour.

They had not hit the blockhouse, they had just churned the sand all around it.

The major might not have been so glum had he known the situation inside the blockhouse. Admiral Shibasaki and his staff were assembled, with a still formidable force of fighting men. But they knew the end was near. At sunset the admiral composed his final message to Tokyo.

"Our weapons have been destroyed. From now on everyone is attempting a final charge. Banzai!"

Not in this big fortress, but in the ruins of the hospital dugout that had been burned out, Petty Officer Oonuki had awaked to find himself—surprisingly—still alive.

He was surrounded by the dead, bloated bodies of his comrades. As he worked himself clear, he heard voices in English. He looked out the hole in the pillbox and saw the superstructure of a ship moving.

By the time that Admiral Shibasaki was composing his last message, Oonuki had regained enough strength so that the instinct for survival returned. He decided to escape to the island of Bairiki, and so as soon as it was dark he had dug a hole and buried his clothes in the pillbox, and then crept out. He had made his way, staggering, toward the end of the island nearest Bairiki. He saw many shapes and shadows in the wreckage of the palm trees and the buildings. He knew they were enemy. He crept more cautiously, and although he was fired at, he was not hit.

At the end of Betio, he had stepped off into the cool water, not more than 3 feet deep, and begun wading across the reef to the other side. Halfway across he saw a figure, and somehow sensed that it was Japanese. He did not make a sound or try to catch up to the other. He just moved ahead, slowly, toward his haven.

Half an hour after moonrise he had reached his goal. He

stepped ashore on the beach, found a bunker, and stepped inside, expecting to find friends there. They were there, but they were not alive. The room was full of charred corpses, victims of marine flamethrowers, men who had died as horribly as his companions in the pillbox back on Betio.

He was sick.

There was only one way out, he decided. The marines were here too, and there was no escape. He must commit suicide. He looked around for something to cut his wrists. He found nothing at all but a seashell. He picked it up and began scraping his wrist, but it was not sharp, enough to cut.

He began to cry. He dropped the seashell and sank down. In a few seconds he was asleep.

Out in the lagoon on the evening of the second day, in one of the tipped, tortured amphibious tractors that had received a direct shell hit from the shore in the early minutes of the battle, there was a stirring. The amtrac was a gory hellhole; parts of bodies lay everywhere. On one side, seeking whatever shelter it gave him, lay a single marine, alive. He had shrapnel in his arms, his legs, his head. He was suffering from thirst and hunger and shock. It was a wonder his wounds and the heat of the Betio sun had not killed him yet.

He and his buddy had been the only two survivors of the whole amtrac full of marines. And his buddy had lasted just until the end of D-Day.

And now it was the second night.

All day long, when he was conscious, the marine had heard the sounds of gunfire, the popping of the Japanese rifles and the sputter of the Nambu machine guns, then the roar of the bigger guns. The whine and the scream of planes coming in, the whirring and the blast of bombs and big shells from the ships. But it did not mean anything—it was all a crazy quilt. All that meant anything was the sun and the heat, and pain.

That night he felt he could not go on. He could not see. His eyes were clotted over with dried blood from his wounds. He knew his throat was on fire, and he hurt everywhere.

He found his rifle, pointed it at his face, and tried to pull the trigger. He was too weak to manage. He fell back in the darkness in the cooling amtrac and he slept.

When Colonel Edson reached the command post on Tarawa at 8:30 that night of the second day, he and Colonel Shoup began making plans for the next day's attack.

First of all, they could use some big-gun support from the sea. So they asked the navy to fire on the eastern end of Betio, keeping 500 yards ahead of the friendly troops. This meant they had to confine their firing to the eastern third of the island.

Strong Japanese fortifications still lay ahead, particularly before the positions inland from Red One and Red Two, where the marines had pushed ahead.

There were also some well-defended places inland from the Burns-Philp pier.

But by this time the superiority of the American military might had begun to count. The Japanese were deserted on their atoll, left to die by a high command that had invoked the spirit of the Emperor (and apparently even his words) in Admiral Shibasaki's blockhouse. They had no more guns, ammunition, or men than before—they had virtually nothing left with which to fight. And by this time all of them knew it.

The Americans were moving tanks, halftracks, machine guns, flamethrowers, artillery, and more men in.

The marines brought guns onto nearby Bairiki, from which they could join in the shelling of the Japanese on Betio.

At 6:00 on the morning of November 22, the third day, the destroyers moved around until they could open up on the "tail end" of the island, where the Japanese were now concentrated.

They were shooting at the big blockhouse where Admiral Shibasaki had taken refuge under the cover of the diversion staged by Petty Officer Oonuki and the others. So a hail of 5-inch naval gunfire, a hail of 75mm howitzer fire, and everything else that could be thrown at the enemy was concentrated on this area.

Half an hour after the bombardment began, the planes began to move in on the end of the island, dive bombers screaming in, and then fighters coming down to strafe. But they could do little against the double logs and concrete of the defenses. It took a direct hit and a lucky one at that from a 1,000-pound bomb to blow up a blockhouse of the Tarawa type.

At 7:00, the First Battalion of the Eighth Marines attacked on the west, supported this day by three light tanks. A tank would move up to a pillbox and fire pointblank into the openings. Then marines would throw in grenades and dynamite charges and other marines would move in with flamethrowers.

But the Japanese continued to fire their own 37mm guns and their machine guns, with good effect against the light tanks that came up so bravely. The tanks and some other vehicles also fell victim to mines. The Japanese had sowed 3,000 small contact mines on the south and west beaches.

But the marines had more resources today. The extension of the beachheads and the wiping out of much of the Japanese power had brought about a new situation. The tanks could land, the gunners were no longer getting killed. Jeeps could come in, and halftracks too, and self-propelled guns with armor shielding. And they came.

Early that morning, there was a certain relaxation at the command post. Colonel Edson and Colonel Carlson and others who had been through the South Pacific could compare this battle to Guadalcanal. It was far worse, they all agreed, and Carlson said it was the toughest fighting he had seen in thirty years, which went back to service in World War I and a sojourn with the Chinese Communist Eighth Route Army.

Those in the command post had the feeling that the officers were now talking of the battle in the past tense. Even though the guns were booming and the machine guns rattling, and there were still many shots to be fired, the officers sensed that the battle was won and the island taken. Even twenty-four hours earlier, the bets might have been hedged more than a little bit.

Even then the marines had fighting to do, and it was proved

when one of the self-propelled 75mm guns was knocked out by Japanese fire that holed its radiators.

This battalion had tough going. The Japanese contested every position, and the main effect of their fight was not so much to gain ground as to kill enemy troops. The Japanese even staged a counterattack in this area of Red One and Red Two strongpoints, and they were beaten back at a frightful toll. But at the end of the day they were still fighting, even though surrounded by the marines.

The big difference on D + 2 was the First Battalion of the Sixth Marine Regiment.

Major Jones launched his attack at 8:00 in the morning. It was led by three light tanks, with the infantry coming up 50 yards behind. A Japanese rushed forward, threw himself under a tank, and pulled the pin on his grenade. It exploded, he died, but the grenade did not even knock the tread off the tank.

The infantry protected the tanks and the tanks forged ahead to assault the blockhouses and other posts from pointblank range. The flamethrowers were at work, too.

This system worked well for the Americans. The Japanese blockhouses became death traps from which there was no escape. In the course of about three hours one marine unit killed 250 of the defenders, and moved ahead to make contact with the First Battalion of Second Marines.

And still there was a war going on. From offshore that morning, a destroyer's shell found an undiscovered fuel dump in the middle of the island, and the whole erupted in a great greasy gout of flame and smoke.

At Colonel Shoup's command post, a sniper edged his way around to flank, and suddenly everyone was hitting the dirt except Shoup, who was yelling at his men to get the sniper.

Prisoners were being captured now—almost all of them Korean laborers as it turned out, men who had been dragged from their homes in Korea to come and work for their Japanese masters. They were glad to give up—they had no loyalty to the Japanese and were pleased to be alive, in a war that was meaningless to them.

By this time, the marines had more on their minds than survival. Those who were not actually involved in the fighting stopped to examine the Japanese fortifications they had broken down. Some of them went souvenir hunting. Correspondent Johnston, traveling with Correspondent Sherrod for the moment, thought he might have a look into a Japanese pillbox, and found a flashlight. But one smell of the interior, where the enemy had died in smoke and flame, disabused him of the notion. He backed out and gave it up.

Now the correspondents and others could look around. Sherrod came to the barracks buildings on the higher ground behind the beaches. He saw in this area atop the seawall the half-sunken machine-gun nests, every 5 yards, little coconut forts shaped like Ys, with the tops half closed, covered with sand and concealed by palm fronds. He could understand why the marines had suffered so badly in going ashore across the reef in the open, unprotected from this fire.

He looked into one pillbox and found four dead Japanese sailors and two dead marines. And that told the story. In those first desperate hours there had been only one way to get at the Japanese, and that was to get in and kill them, which usually meant getting killed oneself in the process. But enough marines had given their lives to let the beachhead live.

The sniping continued even in this area that had been cleaned out hours ago. The Japanese still fought. In one foxhole they found a pair of dead Japanese—dressed in marine jackets and helmets. They had picked up the enemy's gear, all the better to ambush and snipe him down.

There was still plenty to be done.

Major Jones was told that he must continue the attack to the east at 1:00 in the afternoon, to wipe out a stubborn Japanese pocket. That would end Japanese resistance on the whole western half of Betio. To do the job he would take one medium tank and seven light tanks, and he would have naval gunfire and fire from the 75mm guns on Betio and Bairiki. And when this was done, with the help of the Eighth Marines, the Eighth would be allowed to rest after two solid days of fighting.

Major Crowe had reorganized his troops for the attack. His problem was that he was faced with a whole series of strongpoints that must be reduced before he could get anywhere. One of these was a steel pillbox near the Burns-Philp pier. Another was a coconut-log stronghold which was apparently swarming with Japanese machine gunners who kept the company before them pinned down.

As if that were not enough, a third position had to be taken too, the bombproof concrete and log blockhouse south of the others. Crowe still did not know it was Admiral Shibasaki's command post.

The Japanese had designed these three positions to be mutually supporting, and the fact that they had held out this long was a tribute to the planning. They had overlapping fields of fire, and they had so far been able to resist all that the marines could throw against them.

But this day, Crowe had a few extra weapons. He had mortars and tanks, and men who knew how to use explosive charges to rout the enemy out of their boxes.

At 9:30 the mortars opened up on the log bastion. One mortar shell made a lucky hit on the roof and fired off a small ammunition dump there. The bunker virtually exploded. And that was the end of one.

Marines brought a medium tank up against the steel pillbox, and the tank shot several 75mm shells against the structure. One penetrated. That was enough. It quieted the steel box, and let the infantry advance.

Strike two.

The destruction of Shibasaki's bombproof shelter, concrete and coconut log, called for specialists. Up came the infantrymen and engineers, led by Lieutenant Bonnyman. The riflemen kept the Japanese gunners inside pinned down, and Bonnyman and five men with flamethrowers and demolition charges came forward under the covering fire. They managed to get to the top of the structure, the highest point on the island, 17 feet above sea level, although the Japanese were still inside in strength.

When the enemy found the Americans on top of them, they staged a desperate counterattack. It might have succeeded, but for Lieutenant Bonnyman, who turned his gun on the Japanese, killed several, and drove the others back. He fell and rolled down the slope, killed, but the end of the shelter was in sight.

Bonnyman's men rushed up with charges and dropped them in the air vents. With the failure of their counterattack, the Japanese began to run out the east and south entrances to the pillbox, and the marines were waiting for them. They gunned them down with rifles, machine guns, and 37mm antitank guns. A howitzer fired a round of canister. Twenty Japanese fell dead.

Crowe and his men surged around the bombproof shelter, and marines poured cans of gasoline down the air vents and dropped in lighted matches. With a loud roar the whole interior was aflame, and the men inside—150 of them—were broiled. Almost without doubt Admiral Shibasaki was one of them, but so ghastly was what remained that he was never identified.

The way was open now. Crowe and his men did not know it, and so they could not tell Colonel Edson or General Smith, but the Japanese commander was gone, and organized resistance on Betio was ended.

The Second Battalion of the Eighth Marine Division moved out.

Behind them came bulldozers, and one stopped to push sand into the openings of the pillbox. Any Japanese left inside were going to stay there. They were sealed in.

Bulldozers, tanks, the modern machines of modern war: they made all the difference this day.

The battle for control of Betio had begun with the Japanese in a better position than anyone had foreseen. The reason, of course, was that the tanks had been stranded on the reef, and many of the ones that made it in partway were sunk in potholes. The bulldozers could not come in at all in the beginning, and suffered the same fate as the tanks. Jeeps did not make their appearance, or halftracks, or self-propelled guns. The reef had brought the Americans ashore at a distinct disadvantage in spite of their superiority of equipment. The naval guns and the air bombardment had not been nearly so effective against these strong fortifications as they had expected. And so for the first day the Americans hung on by their teeth, and the second by their hands, until the tide was turned by the process of attrition, by the coming of a few fresh troops, but mostly by the ability of the Americans to put their mechanical weapons into action.

The Japanese had underestimated the power of those weapons. Now the Americans were in control of the island, and all that was left for the Japanese was death or surrender.

The Third Battalion of the Sixth Marines had spent the night of November 22 in boats near the line of departure that led to the reefs. Just before 9:00 in the morning they came in, after negotiating the reef with some difficulty. But at least they were not under deadly fire the way the first marines had been on D-Day. They had easy going as they moved along the south coast, and that was a sign of the way the battle was progressing.

General Julian Smith landed from the *Maryland* at 5:30 in the afternoon to set up his command post. He had come ashore just before noon, and looked around Green Beach, but then he had decided to move to Red Two, where Colonel Shoup had his command post.

He quickly enough had an indication that the battle was not over. The best way to get from Green Beach to Red Two was by amphibious tractor by water over the reef. But even this was still dangerous. Japanese on the boundary between Red One and Red Two began firing at the vehicle, wounded the driver, and disabled the amphibious tractor so that the general and his staff had to transfer to another.

By evening the marines could assess the situation coolly. They held two-thirds of the island, and supplies had begun pouring in over the pier by the ton.

The correspondents by this time were eager to get to a ship and begin to write their stories, and even have a bath if they could manage it. Sherrod, Richard Johnston, and Keith Wheeler of the Chicago *Sun Times* found a new cargo-transport ship (an AK) and went aboard. Depending on what they were looking for, they chose either the best or the worst time of all to get off the beach.

For the correspondents had scarcely left before the Japanese staged a counterattack on Betio.

11
BANZAI

Aboard the *Plunger,* Lieutenant Commander Bass was eager to get to some place where he could transship his wounded and the rescued pilot so that they might have adequate medical facilities. A submarine was no place for wounded men if they would be gotten off.

At 2:30 on the morning of November 23 his orders came and he began to move south, headed for Makin to transfer the wounded to proper facilities. It was a great relief.

On the surface they had many air contacts. They knew there were plenty of "friendlies" flying about in these waters, but there should also be a lot of Japanese planes. So the watch was careful.

Just before 8:00 in the morning, they sighted a plane about 7 miles away, and made the proper signals with green flares, green "smokes," and green "comets," but the plane kept coming. That was enough. Bass sounded the alarm, and the *Plunger* plunged.

She did not surface for twenty minutes.

That was the way it went all morning—up and down, surfacing and diving—for either the American planes were paying no attention to the signals, or the Japanese were moving in. They were taking no chances.

At 9:00 the *Plunger* sighted the task force to the south of her, but was forced down by an unidentified plane once more. It was 2:45 before the *Plunger* arrived off Makin and transferred Pilot Brown and the five wounded men to the transport *Leonard Wood.*

Then Bass was able to stop and take stock of the damage to the submarine. They had suffered five 20mm hits and many .25-caliber hits on the bridge, but there was almost no damage except to the high periscope, which had been nicked, scattering black particles over the optics.

The *Plunger* was now able to take advantage of one of the perquisites of the submarine, and the navy in general.

Marines and soldiers, ashore, sweated and stank and ate whatever could be brought to them, usually cold, usually canned. But the navy men had it better. The *Plunger* now took on supplies, fresh fruit, vegetables, the makings of ice cream, all the foods the marines on the beaches dreamed about when the sound of bullets stopped pinging through the air. Theirs was a different kind of war—considered so much more desirable until depth charges began to rain down on a sunken boat, and the seams began to leak.

Here at Makin, the transport *Leonard Wood* gave her supplies, and the ships *Neville* and *Calvert* each gave her three seamen first class to replace the wounded. The flagship *Pennsylvania,* sent over ice cream, candy, and cigarettes.

But by 5:45 that evening it was back to duty, and the *Plunger* was moving out, escorted by the *Revenge* so she would not be in trouble, as the *Nautilus* had been in the early part of the action.

Makin, of course, was now secure, and Howland Smith was on his way to Tarawa.

At Tarawa the victory seemed solid enough, but even as correspondents Johnston and Sherrod soaped in the shower aboard the AK offshore, the Japanese were preparing surprises for the Americans.

The marines had taken the airfield and held most of it—not that at this point it was of any value to the Japanese, who were still being pasted at Mili and other bases by the planes of the carriers.

The Japanese were concentrated in two areas: one called the pocket, which was just that, a pocket of resistance surrounded by marines on three sides and the sea at the back; and the tail end of the island.

The marines knew they would have to rout out the Japanese, and they were preparing to do that the following morning. Colonel Holmes, commander of the Sixth Regiment, had come ashore and established his command post. Next morning he planned to use the Second Battalion of his regiment to support a morning attack by the Third. The Second Battalion was still on Bairiki at that point, finishing the grim business of the day that Petty Officer Oonuki had encountered.

On Betio, Major Jones' three companies held a line across the island from the ocean to the lagoon shore, and that marked the edge of the Japanese positions. B Company consisted of a hundred men, and they had the oceanside flank. They had a new commander, Lieutenant Norman Thomas of Mississippi, who had taken over when the company commander was wounded. At this point in the history of Tarawa there was nothing unusual about that—some units had lost half their men and nearly all their officers, some had lost more. The marines had shown themselves able to cope with almost any sort of changing fighting conditions.

By late afternoon, the marines were dug in, sitting or lying in their foxholes, sometimes picking up an entrenching tool to better the position a little.

Across the way they kept their eyes on the bushes, on the wreckage and the ruined coconut trees that concealed their enemies.

At 7:00 the noises began. The sounds were the noises of animals, baboons and monkeys and wolves and dogs—but there were none of these on the island. There were just Japanese, and the strange noises in the night were an old ploy, known from the days of Guadalcanal: the Japanese were trying to intimidate the enemy. It meant almost undoubtedly there would be some sort of attack.

For the Japanese, the hours were numbered, unless they wanted to surrender. And it was a part of their bushido, their Samurai code, the military system of a nation that was in many ways still half-feudal, that death was far superior to life as a prisoner.

They knew by now that their command post must have fallen, and that Admiral Shibasaki must be dead. They knew that there was no help coming from anywhere, that they were completely overwhelmed by marines and those great ships just off the island. They knew it was time to die. But they did not want to go alone —they wanted to take as many marines with them as they could.

And so at 7:30 it began.

Some fifty howling Japanese rose up out of the brush at the edge of the perimeter and began rushing toward the junction of A and B Companies. They had chosen their point well, for it was here that they were able to break through to the rear.

Lieutenant Thomas was in his foxhole. He heard the noises and the sudden increase in fire as marines shot their weapons at the enemy coming in. He groped for the field telephone.

Then a Japanese with bayoneted rifle leaped into his foxhole and was at him. Thomas grappled with the man, somehow got his .45 loose, shot him in the body, and then blew his head apart to make sure. Then he picked up the telephone and called the command post.

The marines in their foxholes stayed put and fired, and the Japanese fell, for they did not really seek cover but kept moving, looking for their enemies.

When the call came in to Major Jones, he quickly rounded up marines from the headquarters company and the weapons company and sent them forward to drive the Japanese back.

In an hour the fifty were dead. The foxholes were quiet again.

In the calm, Major Jones asked Major Kyles to set up a secondary line from First Battalion of the Second Regiment 100 yards behind the main line. That would prevent a breakthrough if the Japanese tried it again.

And Jones also responded to calls from Lieutenant Thomas for help in the only way he could. He had no men to send in that night, and the companies up front had to hold. But he could get them a bit of fire support, and so he called the navy, and a destroyer was brought up to shell the tail end of the island, to within 500 yards of the marine lines.

Five hundred yards? The marines up front swore it was more like 50, and as the shells came in they wondered just how good the gunners on the ships were.

It was a matter to pray about.

The barrage ended, and at 11:00 the Japanese came again. This time they used more finesse.

A group of some fifty Japanese came up against A Company's perimeter, but they did not come in yelling and shouting and standing up as the others had done so rashly. They shouted a few taunting phrases:

"Marine you die . . ."

"Drink American blood . . ."

"You never go home . . ."

They lobbed in a few grenades.

And then they stopped.

The men of A Company tensed in their foxholes. But when the attack came ten minutes later, it was against B Company.

In the darkness the Japanese came up at a trot, skirmishers, using every skill they had learned in intensive navy training.

In B Company the machine guns opened up. The gunner on one position was killed, and a private came up and took over the weapon. He was Horace Warfield, a Texan.

He had gotten off a couple of bursts when a Japanese jumped into the hole with him and drove a bayonet through his thigh. Warfield grabbed the Japanese and yelled. To his assistance came Marine Private First Class Lowell Koci, who bashed the Japanese in the head with the butt of his rifle and stilled him. Soon the gun was back in action.

The Japanese came after the machine guns. The number-two gunner was killed within minutes of the beginning of the action, but another marine took his place. He was hit but he stayed at the gun, mowing down the Japanese as they came at him.

It was the same at the number-three gun, although the gunner there survived. Though wounded, he kept firing until the shadows drifted away.

It did not take long to beat off this attack. And perhaps, the marines hoped, it was the end of it. How many more Japanese could there be alive in this little bit of real estate?

The Japanese had located the machine guns, and that was part of the plan of the last attack.

They were quiet, for a time.

An hour went by, and then another. More marines began to nod, but then the moon came out from behind the haze and the Americans could see that the Japanese were assembling for still another attack, moving back and forth along the tree line at the edge of their area.

At 3:00 in the morning, fire began to spout out of several wrecked trucks that lay about 50 yards in front of the marine forward positions.

Spotters reported to Lieutenant Thomas that there were two Japanese machine guns there.

The American machine guns opened up on them, but they did not manage to knock out all of the guns—actually, there were more than two. Men from the First Battalion of the Sixth Regiment moved forward and threw grenades into the wrecked trucks. The firing of all but two of the guns stopped then.

At about this time a single Japanese plane came over, making low passes across the island, as if by so doing it could somehow flush out the marines. But no marine moved, and after the second pass, the pilot circled, dropped a handful of antipersonnel bombs that exploded harmlessly near the revetments of the airstrip, and headed out to sea, back for the base he had left.

The marines now knew—with those two machine guns out there sputtering—that the Japanese were not yet finished.

The attack came at 4:00 in the morning, that period of lull when the men's senses seemed even duller than they had earlier. The moon came up and the shadows lengthened, and then came the Japanese—some 300 of them. Some had guns. Some had Samurai swords, some carried knives, and they came charging across the flat, hitting Company B from the front and Company A from the right.

The artillery pulled back to within 75 yards of the front lines, and the destroyers offshore opened up.

The Japanese came on.

Some Japanese were still in uniform, but many were reduced to loincloths, and they made strange fierce figures as they came charging across the sand.

The fighting was as grim as it could be—the Japanese had no hope of survival; their one wish was to kill marines, and then be killed, to achieve honor and valor.

The Japanese came and came and came. But the Americans held fast, and fired at the shadows, and then engaged the yelling, leaping figures and fought with them hand to hand.

At the end of it, in an hour, some 200 Japanese bodies lay outside the marine perimeter. The attack was broken. It was the last one.

12

TARAWA VICTORY

As dawn spread across the island and the sun began to hit the sands, Major Jones' men moved back, and up came the fresh Third Battalion of the Sixth Marines, who were undergoing their baptism of fire.

The problem at this point in the operation was to eliminate the strongpoint between Red One and Red Two, and then capture the tail of the island.

Three separate groups of marines were to undertake the task —the Third Battalion of the Second Marines, the First Battalion of the Eighth Marines, and the Third Battalion of the Sixth Marines, under Lieutenant Colonel Kenneth McLeod.

The new troops had it all their own way. There were an estimated 500 Japanese remaining on the tail of the island, but they were disorganized. Some of them had lost their weapons, they were low on or out of ammunition, and they had no illusions about what fate had in store for them.

They were not willing to give up, but that was as well under the circumstances, for the new troops showed no indication of letting them give up.

This fourth day, the supplies were coming ashore. There were medium tanks and light tanks, and enough flamethrowers to do the grisly job well.

McLeod's battalion began moving out at 8:00 in the morning, and for the first 200 yards it seemed a walk-in—there was virtually no resistance. But then one company came to a group of pillboxes on the lagoon shore, and here it was stalled by machine-gun and rifle fire.

The battle had changed so much in character that at this point, McLeod was able to leave one company to deal with the pillboxes, while he sent the others around its flanks to move ahead toward the end of the island.

So McLeod's effort was really comparatively easy. The Japanese were dispirited and as tired as the marines who had fallen back behind to collapse into sleep; the Japanese defenders would have no such respite.

In a way it was like killing defenseless islanders. "At no time," said McLeod later, "was there any determined defensive. I did not use artillery at all, and called for naval gunfire for only about five minutes, which was all the support used by me. We used flamethrowers and could have used more. Medium tanks were excellent. My light tanks didn't fire a shot."

On this drive to the end of the island, McLeod's marines killed 475 Japanese, and captured fourteen, at a cost of nine marines killed and twenty-five wounded.

When they got to the end, they chased a handful of Japanese across the open water leading to Bairiki, and gunned them down as they tried to find the safety of that island, where there was no safety.

That much was apparent to Petty Officer Oonuki on this morning of the fourth day. Late on the afternoon before, he had encountered four Japanese civilians. They were construction workers who had been caught on the islands, and they had managed, somehow, to move from one place to another and survive the fighting so far.

The civilians told the petty officer that the Americans had already passed by (which he knew very well from the burned bodies in the pillbox) and were working their way up the island chain.

That night they had spent in the surf, wading out into the darkness so they could not be seen from the island and would not encounter any American patrols. They stood there in water up to their waists, all night long, holding onto one another, and they watched the fireworks on Betio. They did not know, of course, that the flashing of guns and the occasional shelling by the destroyers offshore resulted from the attacks of their comrades, those fierce counterattacks of the night before that had wiped out a fifth of the garrison.

At dawn, they had come back to the island and hidden in the bushes of Bairiki, listening to the fighting. All morning long they listened, and they knew by the sounds of the weapons that almost all the firing was being done by the Americans. The end seemed very obvious and very near.

While McLeod's men were moving ever closer to Petty Officer Oonuki and his comrades, two other marine units were having the last of the tough going on Betio. They faced the pocket of resistance on the north shore of the island, a stubborn little force that had been holding out for a day and a half.

Two battalions had the task, the First Battalion of the Eighth Marines and the Third Battalion of the Second Marines. They had extra flamethrowers—which by now they all seemed to agree were the most effective single weapon in reducing the tough Japanese pillboxes.

They had demolition teams from the Eighteenth Marines, and halftracks—self-propelled 75mm guns.

There was very little but small-arms fire against them, and at 10:00 in the morning the units made contact. In the afternoon all opposition on Betio ended.

Sometime around noon the airmen put the seal of finality on it. Down onto the island, buzzing and circling, came a Hellcat with Ensign W. W. Kelly at the controls. He landed on the pocked airstrip and came up to a group of marines.

"Is it over?" he asked.

He already had the answer. If it hadn't been over he would not have been standing there.

In the bushes of Bairiki, Petty Officer Oonuki and the four civilians saw the Hellcat land on the airstrip, and more than any other thing they witnessed, it told them that the battle was all over.

Petty Officer Oonuki's sense of bushido was overcome by his instinct to survive. Wild dreams began to course through his brain. Why could he not steal a boat from the Americans, and in the dark of night make his way through the cordon of great ships? Their very size would help to conceal him. Then once outside, he would trust himself to the mercy of the sea to get him home to Japan.

Two of the civilians obviously thought Oonuki was mad. The other two cautiously said they would go back to Betio with him (for that was where the boats must lie) and at least search for food and water, if nothing else.

They waited for the dark.

The word from "the pocket," which marked the end of the action, was that not a single prisoner had been taken. That in a way summed up the fighting; never had the marines endured so desperate a combat. And now that it was done, there was a general sagging.

General Julian Smith came ashore, conferred with Colonel Edson, and made a short inspection of the area. He then sent a message to Admiral Hill back on the flagship.

The counterattacks of the night before had destroyed almost all enemy resistance. The day's fighting had just about done the rest. He expected complete annihilation of the enemy before the day was over.

There was still some firing. A handful of Japanese defenders were holed up in various hidden positions, with no hope of anything but death, the reward of the Samurai.

As the battle dwindled, there was a feeling that it was all over —so great was the contrast between the comparative quiet of the island and the clatter of guns that had gone on apparently unceasingly for three days.

Offshore, the *Plunger*'s crew was eager to be about what they considered to be the submarine's prime business, sinking the enemy's ships. Captain Bass decided to set his course on the evening of this fourth day for Maloelap, to get back to work.

"Hopes rose that we would soon again hear our torpedoes talking things over with the enemy," he wrote in his log that day.

But before the night was out he had new orders; he was to remain at Mili for observation and rescue services until further notice.

And so that was what the *Plunger* did. For it was not quite all over yet on Tarawa or in the waters around the Gilberts.

The mopping up on Tarawa was easy enough. On the fourth day it was the stink that bothered the men. Some 5,000 dead bodies lay rotting in the sun. The marines could deal with the Japanese rapidly, and they did. The enemy bodies were collected in piles, hauled out to sea in Higgins boats, and dumped into the water. In its way it was not an unfitting end for these sailor-soldiers of an island kingdom.

Robert Sherrod and the other correspondents who had gone to the ships were back, and as the shooting died down to the occasional popping of sniper fire, they wandered about in the wreckage of the island to try to recreate the images of the past few days.

Sherrod discovered that the south beach, which faces into the sea, had been more strongly fortified than the lagoon. Obviously the Japanese had expected the Americans to land there. They had placed rows of land mines in the water and double fences of barbed wire.

On the edge of the airstrip they moved along and examined the fifteen or so Japanese planes, Zeros and twin-engined Betty bombers, all of them damaged by the shelling.

The navy had boasted before the action that it would annihilate Betio with naval gunfire and aerial bombs. But as the correspondents went about, and as Holland Smith came ashore to see the scene of the carnage, they discovered that that promise had not been kept. That had been the trouble—all the basic positions had to be taken by storm, which meant grenades, flamethrowers, and demolition charges. The evidence was there. Most of the pillboxes were sound enough, although full of dead Japanese, many of whom had committed suicide in the knowledge that the end had come.

Among the signs of horror and death there were lessons to be learned about this island, and about the Japanese. After the battle the marines found many 77mm guns quite intact. So much for naval gunfire and bombing: at one tip of the island they found a 5.5-inch gun, set in a concrete cup, the turret hit by many .50-caliber strafing bullets, but the gun quite sound. And there were others, guns ready to fire, only the men who had fired them had been killed.

They found supplies, tons of supplies, food and drink, and stacks of cases of rifle ammunition. The men of Betio had not lacked for anything. The tank traps, the fortifications, were almost unbelievably strong and effective.

That point impressed Holland Smith more than anything else.

General Smith was unaware of it, but he could well have been killed there on the island that day as he was inspecting. Shortly after he and his party passed the west end of the island on the inspection tour, three marines were killed by sniperfire.

No, it was not over for everyone on the fourth day.

It was over for Petty Officer Oonuki that day, however. He and his two civilian companions started back for the shore of Betio late on the night of the fourth day, and on the morning of the fifth in the hours before the dawn they began to edge their way across the shallow water that divided the islands.

Oonuki was halfway across when he stopped to pick some shellfish. He pried them open and ate them there, so hungry he felt he was starving, and his companions left him.

He made it ashore alone, the shellfish making him ill so that he vomited several times. He was so sick he wanted only to find a place to lie down, and he did, just outside a ruined bunker. He fell asleep immediately, to awaken in the glare of the daytime sun, and to see two American marines looking down at him, rifles in hands.

They took him to the rear then—the marines were tired of killing by that time—and someone gave him food and water. He was held in an improvised stockade with the others, mostly Koreans, and a few Japanese. And finally he would be taken to Hawaii and then to a prisoner-of-war camp in Texas, where he would remain until the war ended in 1945.

13
THE *LISCOME BAY*

The Japanese were reeling so hard from the Rabaul carrier strikes that they could not do anything very constructive to aid their troops in the Gilberts.

On November 21 a force of two light cruisers and two destroyers loaded with troops left Truk for reinforcement of the islands, but by the time they reached the Marshalls, Admiral Shibasaki had sent his final message to Tokyo, and they were informed that it was hopeless. They stopped at Kwajalein.

Besides *I-35,* three other submarines moved into the Gilberts area. One of these was *I-175,* commanded by Lieutenant Commander Sunao Tabata. He had been on patrol northeast of the Marshalls when he was called by submarine command at Truk to move into the Gilberts area. By November 23, the fourth day, *I-175* was in the area. She was patrolling off Makin, ordered to do what she could to stop the American invasion, but was kept down for most of the day by four destroyers that seemed to sense that she was about.

To protect the Makin invasion force, Admiral Turner and Admiral Spruance were using an air umbrella provided by three escort carriers. They were in company with the flagship of the fire support group, the *New Mexico,* which was flying the flag of Rear Admiral Robert M. Griffin.

The air group consisted of the escort carriers *Liscome Bay, Coral Sea,* and *Corregidor,* and the unit was under Rear Admiral H.M. Mullinix, who was riding with Captain I.D. Wiltsie in *Liscome Bay.*

These, in turn, were screened by the destroyers *Morris, Franks, Hoel,* and *Hughes,* and the minesweeper *Revenge.*

The little fleet was moving about south of Butaritari, traveling at a leisurely 15 knots, during the hours of darkness. Well before dawn, the order came to get ready for the day's aerial operations, which meant flying at daybreak to support the ships and the troops ashore.

Hoel had been detached for special duty at Makin, which cut down on the screen, but no screen seemed to be needed—the Japanese did not show any signs of serious countermovement against the American attack, certainly not in the Makin area.

Just after 4:30 in the morning, the destroyer *Franks* reported having seen a flashing light, and she was detached from the screen to go and investigate.

At this point Lieutenant Commander Tabata in *I-175* was traveling on the surface, and he saw the force. As dawn was coming soon, he submerged, and began tracking the ships with his periscope.

The *New Mexico*'s radar operators had spotted a blip on the screen that did not seem to belong to anything from the American force. It was *I-175,* on the surface. They watched it for four minutes—then the contact faded and disappeared, as *I-175* submerged.

What was it? The radarmen didn't know.

It might have been a whale. It might have been some ship running off course for a moment. It might have been an aberration of the radar—such was not uncommon in these days, in these climes.

So Admiral Griffin proceeded on course. The ships moved northward, and prepared for flight operations.

At 5:00 in the morning they were about to begin. The three carriers could put up a very effective air cover or strike, with sixteen fighters and twelve torpedo bombers on each of the escorts. Lieutenant Commander M. U. Beebe prepared his pilots for the day's work on *Liscome Bay.*

The early morning was serene then. Up came the destroyer *Franks,* to report that the light appeared to be a flashlight floating on a raft. No people seemed to be on the raft. Anyhow it did not seem to indicate any danger at that moment, although years later naval historian Samuel Eliot Morison was to write that the light was actually a float light dropped by a Japanese scout plane to report to other Japanese aircraft that enemy ships were in the area.

That information was not available to Admiral Griffin, so he did not worry about the light further.

The *Liscome Bay* was at general quarters, a standard procedure before launching planes. Maneuvering to get into the wind for launch, the carriers turned to the northeast and thus just into the path of *I-175.* It was the sort of a target a submarine captain waits for.

Tabata was waiting this morning, and at the proper moment he gave the signal, and *I-175* unleashed the "long lances," the particularly effective Japanese torpedoes which had caused so much havoc in the South Pacific not many months earlier.

Aboard the *Liscome Bay* there was not the slightest indication that anything out of the ordinary was going to occur this morning. Then suddenly the ship seemed to explode.

No one was quite sure what had happened. Some on the bridge said she had taken two torpedoes. But a man in the forward fireroom said he had an impression that three had hit. And that was the feeling of most men who survived.

If so, they struck almost simultaneously, and one or more of them found a vital spot. At least one hit in or very near the bomb stowage compartment, and this meant every bomb there exploded simultaneously.

Men, planes, and fragments of steel from the ship went high in the air, so high that the *New Mexico,* which was traveling nearly a mile behind her, was showered with everything from plating to grisly bits of human flesh and clothing. The whole after portion of the ship simply vanished.

Immediately the ship was aflame from stem to stern, and one blast followed another as some bit of explosive or gasoline was found by the fires.

Two of the destroyers were absent; the officers and men of the others watched in awe as the flames shot up from one end of the flight deck to the other. Ammunition began to explode, sending up gouts of flame as if from a huge Roman candle.

There was really no question aboard the *Liscome Bay* of damage control or fighting the fire. The ship was actually consumed before the eyes of the men who watched.

Those aboard simply tried to save themselves—there was nothing else to do, and even that was difficult enough. The destroyers immediately began moving in toward the carrier. They could not approach it closely because of the flames, but they could make ready. They did not attempt to discover *I-175,* and Lieutenant Commander Tabata escaped.

The destroyer *Morris* moved in as close as possible, and when the *Liscome Bay* finally sank, about fifteen minutes later, the *Morris* moved into the wreckage and put over her motor whaleboat to pick up survivors.

It was a hard job. Just finding the men in the oil was hard enough, and getting them aboard was worse. The wreckage was heavy and hid some men. Of the men in the water, many had oil all over them, including in the eyes, and they could not see their rescuers.

One man, who had been operated on for appendicitis just two days earlier on the carrier, got into the boat, and then asked if they could not give him a rubber boat to go out and rescue some of his comrades.

Electrician's Mate T. R. Furnas of the *Morris* dove repeatedly into the water and rescued grimy, oil-soaked men. It was an old experience for Furnas—he already held the Silver Star for the same kind of rescue work in the sinking of the carrier *Hornet* in the South Pacific.

Lieutenant (J.G.) Loren H. Killion and Ensign Joseph R. Guerrant found a rubber life raft aboard the *Morris* and paddled out through the oil to pick up badly wounded men off a piece of wreckage.

And aboard the destroyer, survivors were taken to the sick bay and the improvised areas, where Lieutenant Commander John D. Rowe of the *Liscome Bay* and Lieutenant (J.G.) Herbert L. Armentrout, the medical officer of the *Morris,* took them in hand.

By this time it was 7:00 in the morning, and the sun was rising higher every moment. The survivors were indescribably filthy with oil. It was hard to determine even the extent of their injuries. Some were badly burned, some suffered broken limbs, some were in shock. Virtually every man was hurt in some way, but those with minor injuries refused to be treated, telling the corpsmen and the doctors to take care of the more seriously hurt people.

And there were many badly hurt. One man died while the medical officers were giving him plasma. Another died as he was being picked up by the *Morris'* motorboat.

Commander F. T. Williamson, captain of the *Morris,* had been through the sinkings of the *Lexington, Yorktown,* and *Hornet,* but he had never seen anything like the sinking of the *Liscome Bay.*

Altogether, fifty-five officers and 217 men were rescued, including Lieutenant Commander Beebe, leader of the carrier's air group. But Admiral Mullinix was never seen again after the bridge began to go, and Captain Wiltsie also went down with the ship, along with fifty-one other officers and 591 enlisted men.

From the group of destroyers screening Admiral Griffin's flagship, the *Gridley* came up to help. The *Morris* reported screw noises while she was in the midst of rescue operations, but they did not seem to make any sense, and Captain Wilkinson decided they had come from U.S.S. *Baltimore,* which was nearby.

But then the *Gridley* had a contact at 1,500 yards, reported by her soundmen, and she went to investigate. The destroyer dropped a full pattern of depth charges. That ended the contact; no more was heard or seen, and the *Gridley* left the scene, without making any claims at all.

Actually, Tabata had kept *I-175* in the area, hoping for another shot, and the run by *Gridley* very nearly did send the Japanese submarine down to the bottom. She was sorely hurt by the depth charging; gauges broke, glass burst, lights went out, and leaks developed. But she turned north and headed for the protection of the air bases at Kwajalein. No one followed her.

As for the rest, it was so quiet a day that it was hard to realize that *Liscome Bay* was gone, and that the Japanese still had a mighty sting.

An occasional victory was not enough to ensure success for the Japanese defense. Admiral Koga had thought to send troops from the light cruisers *Isuzu* and *Naka* from Kwajalein to reinforce the troops on Tarawa particularly. Reinforcement was in the air all along, and Fourth Fleet headquarters, under Vice Admiral Masashi Kobayashi, was transferred to the Marshalls, as if the Japanese were planning a major defensive effort.

But it was too late for the Gilberts. The troops went to Mili when it was learned that the Gilberts had fallen on the 24th.

The heavy cruisers *Jumano, Chokai,* and *Suzuya,* the light cruiser *Noshiro,* and a dozen destroyers hurried to the area, but once again the decision was that it was useless to risk them in a battle that was already lost. So they did not seek engagement from that point, but returned southward in a few days.

Of the submarines that Admiral Takagi had dispatched to the Gilberts area, *I-35* was already sunk, and *I-175* had gotten away, to limp back to the safety of Truk.

I-19, according to Japanese sources (and *I-40,* according to Samuel Eliot Morison), was discovered by the U.S. destroyer *Radford,* of the group screening the carriers that accompanied the Makin force. It was a night contact, on November 25, about 60 miles west of Makin.

Commander Gale E. Griggs had honed his ship to a fine edge of fighting strength, and his radarmen made contact first. Then, when the destroyer moved in, the soundmen took over and found the submarine.

It was a battle of wits for several hours, the submarine turning, twisting, and escaping, to be found again, and the destroyer moving in to make one depth-charge attack after another. On the fourth attack, the destroyer's crew heard a loud underwater explosion in addition to their "tin cans" going off.

It was near midnight, and the surface of these waters told them nothing. But next morning, with the assistance of planes from the carriers, the destroyer located a mass of debris and concluded that she had sunk a submarine.

The *Radford* was awarded a "probable kill," no more. But the fact was that neither *I-19* nor *I-40* ever came home. The commander of one of them, Commander Kobayashi of *I-19*, was one of the more valuable officers in the Japanese navy. He had been responsible for modifying the new torpedo, the "long lance," from 24 inches to 21 inches to fit into the tubes of the submarines.

Besides these, the Japanese lost three other submarines in the Gilberts during the campaign. Records are sparse and there was much guesswork involved until after the war, when American records became available to the Japanese navy, and there was time to reconstruct this period of history.

I-21, under Commander Hiroshi Inada, set out from the big base at Truk on September 25, found for the Fijis, but was diverted to the Tarawa area on November 11 (long after any normal patrol would have ended). The length of the patrol was a certain sign of the Japanese difficulties in maintaining strength even at this early period of the Pacific war. When *I-21* was sent to Tarawa, the crew were already near exhaustion, which meant their capacity for making mistakes was greatly increased.

The submarine set out and made a few radio reports, and then was not heard from after it reached Gilbert waters. *RO-38* was also lost in this operation, after having reached the islands—whether to a plane, or a destroyer, or to some unknown tragedy no one ever ascertained.

14
THE STORM OVER
THE GILBERTS

On November 27, a week after the landings, both atolls were secure. Garrison troops began to land, and the combat troops moved out.

Admiral Nimitz flew in with a train of admirals and generals from Pearl Harbor, to see the first conquest of the Central Pacific campaign.

Spruance moved in to shore to meet them, and for the first time set foot on Betio. The boat took him into the long pier where so many marines had died, where Major Crowe had fought so gallantly with his men. He and his staff went through some pillboxes and learned how ineffective the naval gunfire had been.

They saw the piles of rotting bodies that the marines were still burying in common graves. And for the first time since the Philippines days, Admiral Raymond Spruance had a sense of the death and destruction of the war on land.

The battle won, Spruance was eager to be off and back to Pearl Harbor, for the Marshalls assault was coming too close for comfort: he should be planning the operations. But the fleet had to remain in the Gilberts while the supply ships unloaded their materials for the garrison forces. They would remain for two whole weeks. The fast carriers were released on November 26 and moved out to strike other Japanese bases, to decimate Nippon's air power in readiness for the coming Marshalls invasion.

Spruance began evaluations, preparing to write his action report, which would go to Nimitz, and then to King. The whole story must be told; on the telling might depend Spruance's future.

It was apparent that many mistakes had been made. Kelly Turner wrote Spruance about the difficulties at Makin. It all boiled down to the incompetence of the Twenty-seventh Division, the national-guard outfit, which Turner said was the least effective of the four national-guard divisions with which he had been associated in operations against the Japanese.

The trouble was the leadership. It was as simple as that.

And if Turner was restrained, Holland Smith was almost incoherent on the subject. He made serious complaints about the Twenty-seventh Division and its officers. He had small use for General Ralph Smith, and he was at very little pains to conceal the fact. His wrath was felt, and known, and at army headquarters resentments began to rise.

And then, back at Pearl Harbor, the postmortems began. It was Nimitz' habit to hold postmortems on military actions, and the Gilberts was to be no exception.

Holland Smith spoke up and said that in his opinion the whole bloody show had been a waste of time and men's lives. This was the position also taken by the airmen of the navy, who had never believed the Gilberts invasion was essential. They had been sure from the beginning that a strike at the Marshalls, after knocking out Japanese air power, would speed the war along.

For, in spite of Admiral King's statement earlier that the capture of the Gilberts was "a necessary part of any serious thrust at the Japanese Empire," marines and airmen said Tarawa had no particular strategic importance, and as a base it was of virtually no value. It constituted no threat to communications in the South Pacific, there were no dock or naval facilities, the airfield was little more than a staging field, and to have ignored it would have hurt nothing.

The facts were harder and crueler. The reality was that the Gilberts operation was "training," and little more than that. Nonetheless it was essential, for until the Americans had been trained, until the Fifth Fleet had been welded into a fighting force, it might have been suicidal to send it against a stronger bastion.

Many marine lives were sacrificed, nearly 1,000 of them, and more than 2,000 men were wounded in the battle for Tarawa. But their sacrifice paved the way for the whole drive across the Central Pacific.

The battle of the Gilbert Islands ended officially on November 24, but not for the aviators of the fleet.

They had been straining for days to be gone and on their way to the Marshalls to hit the big Japanese air concentrations there, particularly at Kwajalein. The young Turks on their carriers and Admiral Towers back at Pearl Harbor claimed that the way to defeat the Japanese was to knock out their air power on the ground or as it arose from the bases to meet the carrier threat.

During the Gilberts battle the Japanese had been able to mount only two air offensives, on the 20th and the 27th. In the first, they hit the *Independence*. In the second, on the night of November 27, they came in, perhaps a hundred of them, and they separated to find the carriers, which were their main targets. Some thirty torpedo bombers settled on Admiral Radford's Task Group 50.2, the *Enterprise*, the *Belleau Wood*, and the *Monterey*.

Knowing that the Japanese liked to attack just after dark, Admiral Radford had already begun night training (which would eventually provide for the fleet a night carrier which launched night fighters). This night, Lieutenant Commander E. H. ("Butch") O'Hare, who had already won the Congressional Medal of Honor for his air exploits, led two other night fighters up to break up the attack. The planes did so, and shot down several, but O'Hare was lost as well.

Next day the Japanese struck again—land-based air from the

Marshalls once more. This time Admiral F. C. Sherman's destroyer screen drove off the Japanese planes by gunfire.

The carrier men had a lesson in something they already knew: keep the carriers out past the point of operations for land-based air, or plan to run into trouble.

But the carriers' doctrine was the same: hit the enemy hard before he could hit you. And that is what they set out to do in the Marshalls to soften the islands up for the coming invasion.

On December 4, they were in position to launch, with six carriers, under overall command of Admiral "Baldy" Pownall. They began sending off the fighters and bombers at 6:00 in the morning.

On that day, the Americans arrived over Kwajalein to discover a fleet of more than two dozen Japanese warships in the anchorage. This was the force assembled to fight for the Gilberts, but too late.

The Hellcats and the torpedo planes attacked. They plastered the anchorage and sank several ships, and made a hit on a cruiser. They attacked Japanese planes on the ground. They engaged in a running battle in the air, shot down eighteen Japanese fighters and nearly a dozen bombers, and lost several planes in return.

When they got back to their carriers, they had the word from Admiral Pownall:

Cancel operations.

He wanted to "get the hell out of there," as Halsey had said much earlier about a similar raid on Japanese territory, but the Halsey raid had been at the beginning of the war, with a single carrier, and now there were six. It was a different story, but "Baldy" Pownall did not see it that way.

The young Turks were itching for a fight; they knew there were scores of Japanese planes on the airfields back in the Marshalls, and they wanted to knock them out right then.

Pownall refused. He insisted on moving the carriers out of "danger," leaving enemy bombers unhurt at Roi and Wotje and on Kwajalein. They did make a strike on Wotje and knocked out half a dozen torpedo bombers on the ground. But that afternoon other bombers approached. They were the planes left unhurt by the carrier strikes, and one of them managed that night to put a torpedo into the carrier *Lexington.* The torpedo damaged her stern, jammed her rudder, and killed several men and wounded others.

It never would have happened, said the young Turks, if they had been allowed to raid and reraid the Japanese bases in the Marshalls all that day.

And so, when the ships and the men reached Pearl Harbor after this raid, the young Turks were geared up for trouble. Captain J. J. Clark rushed up to Nimitz' headquarters with aerial photographs taken by his planes, showing all the Japanese bombers and fighters left untouched on the airfields. And that word was quickly passed to Rear Admiral C. H. McMorris, Nimitz' chief of staff.

It would create its own small volcano at the Pacific Fleet headquarters.

When General Holland Smith got back to Pearl Harbor he had many unkind words for the navy, and particularly the manner in which his men had been landed. The highly vaunted naval bombardment had been a dismal failure in knocking out the Japanese prepared positions. The air bombardment had been no better, ragged and uneven; only where a direct hit was scored on a structure did it knock it out. Ensign Kiyoshi Ota, now a prisoner of war, was open in admitting that the bombardments had played hob with the Japanese communications. But important as this was, it was not what had been intended or sought: when the unknown voice on the bridge of the *Maryland* had predicted that there would not be fifty Japanese alive on the island as the marines went in, he had been stating a general belief.

Some 3,000 marines, the dead and the injured, were testimony to how little effect the naval guns and air bombs had had.

As for the tides, the navy wrote the matter off as "calculated risk," and there was not really much that could be said about that. It was certainly true that the possibility of an extra low tide had been noted, but had been dismissed as so unlikely as to be beneath consideration. But had it not been for Holland Smith's absolute insistence that they use the amtracs—a battle he had fought right up the line to Spruance, after a mighty tussle with "Terrible Turner"—then the marines might not have gotten ashore at all, and the Gilberts, instead of being a heroic disaster, would have been a disastrous fiasco. Without those amtracs, without the heroism of the marines at Tarawa, the entire course of the Central Pacific campaign might have been changed. Indeed, with the pressure from MacArthur and the army, the whole Pacific war might have been bogged down or even diverted with failure at the Gilberts.

For the army was furious. If Holland Smith had unkind words for General Ralph Smith and the Twenty-seventh Division, Ralph Smith, reporting back to General Richardson, had even more stinging rebukes for the indelicacies heaped upon him by a "goddam marine."

In no time at all the story had gotten to Washington, where General Arnold and General Marshall certainly did not take the navy or marine point of view.

"Terrible Turner" wrote Nimitz about the deficiencies of the army men, and "Howling Mad" Smith spoke up loudly and frequently about his own views.

So the dispute simmered. Eventually it would boil over; "Howling Mad" would relieve Ralph Smith in the heat of battle for all the same reasons he was displeased at the Gilberts. Out of it all would come a long struggle, and in the end, at Okinawa, the army would take over the land battles, and (privately) army generals would say that never again would they serve under the command of a marine general.

The quarrel between "Baldy" Pownall and his young Turks would simmer, too, but not for long. When Nimitz saw the pictures of the "birds that got away" on the airfields of the Marshalls, he came to the reluctant conclusion that Admiral Towers and the aviators were right in this case. Admiral Pownall was simply not aggressive enough to lead the carrier forces into battles. And so it was done in a hurry: "Baldy" Pownall was relieved, and a hard-bitten aviator of the tough and aggressive school, Admiral Marc Mitscher, was put in charge of the carrier force. The aviators were well satisfied, for in Mitscher they had a real flier, an old squadron commander, a pilot who thought like a pilot, and not a retread battleship man who got his wings just to qualify to run a carrier.

Towers won this much for his aviators, but he did not manage to get his own command. Admiral Spruance, showing that cool detachment that had made him famous at the Naval War College, stood above it all, almost on the level (but never quite) of Nimitz himself, and Spruance surveyed the quarreling beneath him.

He hated quarrels; he found it easier to ignore them and if they kept emerging, to force his chief of staff or someone else to deal with them. He had long operated on the principle that if one ignored troubles, most of them went away, and so he continued.

As far as the amphibious operations were concerned, the costly victory in the Gilberts had taught the navy much that its commanders, officers, and men needed to know. The team that was forged here, with "Terrible Turner" in charge, and Harry Hill to assist him, would perform nobly in future landings. The marines had learned how difficult the going could be in this island hopping, and they would have the same experience time and again in the future. There was no easy way to end this war, and above all else that is what the Storm over the Gilberts had taught.

NOTES AND BIBLIOGRAPHY

Much of the research for this book was done in the Classified Archives section of the U.S. Naval History division in Washington Navy Yard. I am indebted to Dr. D. W. Allard, Mrs. Kathy Lloyd, and many other members of the staff there for favors and assistance time and again.

The basic documents of the Gilberts campaign are the action reports of the various commands and vessels which participated. I used all these. I also used a number of other sources, some of them from my own *How They Won the War in the Pacific* (Weybright and Talley, 1969).

Admiral J. J. Clark's *Carrier Admiral* was valuable in giving an insight into the story of the aviators. Also, much earlier, I had the use of the papers of the late Admiral Jack Towers, through the courtesy of his widow. Towers gave very definite opinions about the course of events at this period of the war.

Samuel Eliot Morison's *History of United States Naval Operations in World War II, Vol. VII,* is the standard starting work. It was valuable for many clues and some detail.

The Amphibians Came to Conquer, the Story of Admiral Richmond Kelly Turner, by Vice Admiral George C. Dyer, USN Ret., is also important in giving much detail about planning and naval operations, including a clear view of what went wrong with the tidal prognostications at Tarawa and why.

The History of the U.S. Marine Corps Operations in World War II, by Shaw, Nalty, and Turnblad (Central Pacific Drive), is also important—vital for the account of the marines in operation. The action reports of the V Amphibious Corps also give a good deal of the detail, although some of them have been subject to correction in recent years.

Thomas B. Buell's *The Quiet Warrior,* a biography of the late Admiral Raymond A. Spruance, was useful. More useful to me was my own long interview several years ago with Rear Admiral Carl Moore (USN Ret.), who had been Spruance's chief of staff.

Martin Russ' *Line of Departure, Tarawa* told a good deal of detail about Japanese operations, as did Zenji Orita's *I-Boat Captain.* I also secured some information on this subject from the reports of questioning of Japanese naval officers by the Strategic Bombing Survey Team at the end of World War II. Further, some materials, translations from the Japanese, were available in the naval archives.

Other sources for my discussion of the battle at Tarawa were my old friend Robert Sherrod, whose book *Tarawa, the Story of a Battle,* has never been surpassed for giving the sheer horror of war, and Richard W. Johnston, another old friend, who was also there, and who from time to time has told me tales about it over the past thirty years.

Holland Smith's *Coral and Brass* tells his views and activities during the battle, although it is greatly submerged in the train of events that followed in the Pacific war.

W.J. Holmes' *Undersea Victory* gives a capsule view of the activities of the American submarines in the area in the period.

Charles Bateson's *The War with Japan* is useful for setting background.

The story of the Makin raid by Evans Carlson and his raider battalion is part of a tale as yet unpublished, which I wrote several years ago for a publishing house now defunct.

But the backbone of this book is in the papers, the action reports and interviews, and the war diaries that were made in or just after the heat of battle. They and the personal stories of the participants are essential factors in this book.

INDEX